Justin Time

Autobiographical Stories from an American Spiritual Master

J. Jaye Gold

Peradam Press
North San Juan, California

Peradam Press
P O Box 6
North San Juan, California 95960
peradam@earthlink.net

A division of The Center for Cultural & Naturalist Studies, Inc.

Book design and cover: Chela
Transcribing Coordinators: Pranavati & Hope
Editorial Proofreading: Johanna & Renee

Library of Congress Cataloging-in-Publication Data

Gold, J. Jaye, date
Justin Time : Autobiographical stories from an American spiritual master / J. Jaye Gold
p. cm.
ISBN 978-1-885420-02-2
Includes biographical reference, table of contents, preface, and prologue.
1. Non-fiction. 2. Spiritual. 3. Biography. 4. Psychology.
I. Title. II. J. Jaye Gold

Library of Congress Control Number: 2016957041

Printed in the United States of America
9 8 7 6 5 4 3 2 1

Author's Note

When I was a kid, I was a picky eater. I had a lot of *yeses* and *nos* in my eating. I was more or less catered to in that, because I'd throw food on the floor if I didn't get what I wanted. One of the foods I wouldn't eat was peas. If peas were on a plate that I was given, it didn't matter if the other things on the plate were my favorite things, all I would say is, "I don't eat peas. I don't eat peas. I don't eat peas." And I wouldn't eat it.

Why wouldn't I eat everything else on the plate? It doesn't make sense, but I wouldn't do it. If there were peas on the plate, I became fixated on those peas – I would get stuck there, and everything else became unacceptable to me. I have since transcended that limitation, and through years of working on myself, I have come to even liking peas. So there's hope for all of you in the ditches that you've dug.

This is my advice to you in reading this book. You may come across something that gives you trouble – peas. Try not to get hung up on it, because the next thing might be something that you find really interesting, and may even present an idea that's a new direction for you. It may even be something that has eluded you over the years. Some things that I have written may be contrary to thoughts that you've had before. This is possible, and even probable, so try not to get stuck, and as I say, and as others have said, take what you can and leave the rest.

Introduction

Several of my capacities have been officially acknowledged by branches of national, state, and local governments. Five states have acknowledged my ability to drive a motor vehicle. I was granted a passport by the Department of State of the United States when I was twelve years old. I have, in the past, held a real estate license in Maryland, Washington, D.C., and Virginia, and was at one time certified as an emergency medical technician EMT-2 by the State of California. If that's not enough for you to enter chapter 1, after which I believe necessity for my bona fides would be moot, you can refer to the last chapter in this book, but I would rather you left those words to be read in the order I presented them. They were placed last for a reason. And, oh yes, I neglected to mention – in my close to seventy years on this earth, in addition to the above, since 1980, I have been an unlicensed and unaccredited spiritual friend, teacher, guide, master and guru to hundreds of people.

Preface

My first name is Justin – a name that I like enough to have never considered changing it, and one that I am called by my friends. I only use the name J. Jaye Gold because I share the name Justin Gold with someone who occupies the first hundred references on Google and all other search engines. He makes the *choke*, in *choke and slide,* and though I do respect his business accomplishments, I am choosing to keep our fields of endeavor distinct. My middle name is however unique, and to avoid confusion, I have coined that as my brand.

The title is a cute play on words using my name, but it is much more than that. You see, I was one of the first Justins. This latest profusion of Justins, one that causes my head to be constantly jerking around to see who is calling me, started much later. In my youth, my first name was an oddity, and being so, I was subject to the teasing of my peers. Justin Time was one of the names that I was called. The spiritual life does not afford many opportunities for retribution, nor would it be appropriate, so I have waited a long time for requital – an opportunity to use the clever pun of my childhood as an implement to attract the attention of anyone who would care to read what life is like in Justin Time.

I have written this book using Microsoft Word on a HP computer that was given to me for a recent birthday. It came from Costco, and probably cost somewhere around 700 dollars. It has a backlit keyboard and a touchscreen, but otherwise is a standard piece of equipment. There are certainly more state-of-the-art computers, but this one had all I needed to write and organize words on a page in a document, so a more sophisticated computer would clearly have been overkill for my purposes.

I got another birthday gift many years before that. It was for my actual birthday – the day I was born. It was a human body. It contains such a bounty of sophisticated state-of-the-art, never fully utilized equipment, that I have spent a lifetime trying to figure out, "Why so much technology? What's it all for?" I could have done just as well with a basic model. Many of my species do little with similar equipment other than eat, sleep, procreate, and do various physical and mental tasks. Why so much for so little?

Why would a species with so much equipment for analysis, deliberation, and the acquisition of reason, remain so confused about methods for resolution of basic issues? Why has violence remained an option for such resolution, when it is clear that its effects are pitifully temporary? Why has the quest for wealth and recognition persevered as a solution for a fulfilled life, when there has never been evidence that it works? My purpose in presenting this book is to help *explore* questions such as these and others – not to answer them.

If, along with their benefits, the religious proclamations, scientific discoveries, and spiritual revelations of the past 100 years have decreased the mystery of human life, they have done us a dis-service. This book is neither religious, scientific, nor is it spiritual – it is a primer for exploration, written by one who has dedicated his life to the endeavor of studying that mystery.

I am no Hemingway, no Steinbeck, no James Joyce, nor do I claim to be the possessor of the talent of the likes of these. My art form is that of perspective and humor derived from an altitude that allows both impartiality and compassion. The stories that follow are taken from my life, and I have chosen them because they reflect that unique capacity.

This is not a how-to book, nor is it a self-help manual – that type of book should be relegated to carpentry, auto repair, and cooking. When it comes to the uncovering of the spirit, following instructions in a book without someone looking over your shoulder, making sure you are interpreting them correctly, would be about as reliable as reading road directions in a foreign language, and guessing which direction to turn.

Table of Contents

Chapters

Dedication

To Jack, my father, who constructed the door that I might walk through, and Raya, who was there when I did.

The words in this book are the product of a collaborative effort between everyone I have ever crossed paths with and myself. How could it be otherwise? I act as their proxy in putting down on paper all that follows, and thrust it into the future that begins now.

Other books by J. Jaye Gold:

Another Heart in His Hand
Highway of Diamonds
The Roca Group

Chapter 1
Hope and Expectation

New York City was the place where our planet's creative forces converged to broadcast and receive the world's first television programs. I was really young when television started. I lived in an apartment building with 70 or 80 apartments, and our family had the first TV set in the building. It had a ten-inch screen, but there was a magnifying glass that you could slide on the front of the TV screen to enlarge the picture. These days you might see one of them in a Salvation Army thrift store – more likely in an antique store.

My grandmother, who was a *hosty* kind of person, would set up chairs theater style in the living room for anyone in the building who wanted to come and watch the TV. There were only one or two stations at the time, and only a few shows – mostly between six and nine at night. I would sit in anticipation in front of the TV a couple of hours in advance, already having the feeling of the limitless possibilities connected with the miracle that I was about to witness.

I was anxious about the seating because I was smaller than everybody else who came to watch, and if I didn't get a good seat, I wouldn't be able to see. If you sat too close to these magnifiers, you also couldn't see much. So I would stake out my seat when everybody else was eating dinner. I would be in the front row, just sitting there watching the blank screen, with all of my hopes, aspirations, and dreams primed to unfold within an hour. My family would call me to come to dinner, but after a while they gave up and served me right where I was. That was the inception of the TV table. It should actually have been called the Justin table, like a Martin desk, or a Stickley chair. I would sit in front of the TV without budging. My expectations were so high, that I couldn’t risk losing this most preferable seat for watching my hopes come to life.

The way I see it, there are three categories of hope and expectation. My initiation into the world of TV is a story about maximum hope – *I‘ve got to get there early.* Then as expectations drop down a little, there is the second category, which could be described as, *I don't want to be late*. Then as you descend some more, you eventually get to, *What's it matter when I get there?*

What are the components and the variables that cause our expectations to devolve, from wanting to be early, to not caring when we get there? I'm feeling my six-year-old self sitting there looking at that TV, looking at that magnifying glass – sitting in that chair with the little table in front of me not really interested in the food on it – just thinking, *How much time now*? *How much time now*? I was recognizing the possibility that there was something magical that was going to come to me – something that was going to cure whatever emptiness a six-year-old's life can contain. I had hope. I had hope that something would be there for me.

And then sometime later on, after the magnifying glasses had come off, and I'd already put in hours and hours in front of this *magic box*, even though I continued to watch TV, I realized that it wasn't going to do it for me. My hopes were ill-founded. I wasn't going to be made okay by the pictures it displayed. It wasn't going to fill the emptiness that this, by then eleven or twelve-year-old boy experienced.

I still didn't want to get there late, I didn't want to *miss* the beginning of the show, but I didn't want to make sure I was there for the beginning. I just didn't want to *miss* the beginning. My hopes had decreased a little. A couple of years after that, it just didn't matter at all. I still needed it. I still showed up. TV still helped me get from one day to the next, but my hopes were gone.

How about the hopes of those of us who have tried to seek something finer, something beyond the ordinary goals of acquisition and comfort – something even reaching toward truth? Most of us are in that category, at least to a modest degree. Even *our* hopes have been downsized from, "I gotta be there, I gotta be the first one there." Now we're at a place where, "I don't want to *miss* this chance," not, "I *want* this chance." I'm sure you can feel the difference.

Chapter 2
Crossing the Sahara

Watching as much TV as I did had numerous effects on me. The most obvious, of course, was the numbness that is the residue of that activity. On the positive side, I did develop a considerable curiosity for travel to foreign places, and along with that, a desire to be something other than a tourist – both qualities that I have to this day.

The value of knowing more than one or two words in the language of a foreign country one is visiting was evidenced to me once again while having my EMT license recertified. While I was putting in the required number of hours in the Santa Barbara Hospital emergency room, a foreign tourist came in looking to get help with a significant problem he was facing – an emergency. He lost his passport. He found his way to my post late at night by taxi, because the only word he could remember of the five he knew in English was *emergency*.

I'm going to tell you a story about how I confirmed the importance of having access to different ways of communicating with people. I'm referring to having different languages available for talking to people, not in this case like French or German, but languages of common experience. My presenting this story to you is in itself an example of a language, because it's a bit of an adventure story, and people like the language of adventure stories – at least most people do. Follow along and you'll get to know how I verified that a person cannot expect to communicate with diverse individuals if they have only one point of reference, because people's lives are varied, and there are so many languages of experience.

Some years ago, several friends and I were involved in adventure traveling to exotic locations. These days, though some of our traveling is still to similar locations, the focus of our trips has evolved more into social work adventures. One of those early expeditions took nine of us to the Sahara Desert in North Africa. Our aim was to cross the Algerian Sahara from far north to deep south, ending up in the Hogar Mountain town of Tamanrasset.

We began by crossing into Algeria from Morocco at a town called Bechar. Algeria is and was an extremely military and regulated country – not an easy country to travel in, nor even to enter. Our numbers made for difficulties at the border, so it was clear that we wouldn't be able to move nine people 500 miles south without considerable attention from the authorities. Our solution was to break into groups of three – a reasonable number of people to hitch, or take buses, or trucks or whatever.

I was healthy, but some of us had gotten sick in Morocco – one person in particular was in a weakened condition. I decided it was best if I take her on, because I saw myself as being responsible for this expedition. So my threesome included one person who was feeling sick and had to be assisted along the way. We started out by hitching and getting rides on commercial trucks that travel the road south. We got about halfway, when she started to feel really bad. We found out later that she had bacterial dysentery and eventually found the right medicine and she got better. But at this time, it was not good. We were dropped off by a truck in Adrar, a town in the middle of the Algerian Sahara.

It had recently been discovered, that under this area was a wealth of natural gas, so it had become a military and commercial installation. There was a lot of action going on in this middle of the Sahara town, which at one time had a population of 1,000, but now had grown to 5,000 – many of whom were military. We were in this town looking for a way to eventually continue south. I say eventually, because to go on immediately was unrealistic, because one of our threesome was clearly unable to do so. We did find some medicine in town, and she was feeling a little better, but very weak.

We spent a couple of days there in a hotel that was hastily constructed for Japanese businessmen that were coming in to buy the natural gas. After a couple of days she was a little better, but still too weak to hitch or truck.

We had heard from somebody, that there was a small plane that sometimes took civilians to Tamanrasset – the town in the middle of the Hogar Mountains where we wanted to go to meet our friends. The plane flew out of the Adrar military base, which was about five miles outside of town.

Our arrangements allowed each group a week to ten days to arrive at our destination. We were going to meet on the main street corner of Tamanrasset. Each day at noon, whoever had made it there, would come into town and see who showed up. We had already used about half of our days, so we had two reasons that we needed to get on the plane that took off from the military base.

My idea, and it wasn't a good one, was to get as close to the military base as we could the night before, and camp there. Then early in the morning, walk onto the base and be the first ones to get on the plane – maybe even arrange it the night before. Our inquiries into getting to the airport were met with locals extremely reluctant to go there. We didn't understand why, but the words were, "You can't go there, you can't go there." We tried to convey, in either French, or Arabic, that we didn't want to go *onto* the military base, we just wanted to go near it to camp. It was still, "No, no, no."

Finally, by offering to pay double or triple the usual amount, we found a cab driver who would take us. He drove us out and dropped us off on the road about half a mile from the military base and turned around and headed back to town. We crossed the road into the dunes and found a place to camp where we couldn't be seen from the road. It doesn't rain there and the nighttime weather is beautiful, so we were fine camping there.

After about an hour of hanging out and munching on our granola bars, we heard vehicles coming, so we slumped down hoping we weren't going to be discovered – but we were discovered. It turned out to be a convoy of four military vehicles, one having a manned machine gun on top, and the others, armored personnel carriers, all coming across the dunes, with little question as to where they were heading. They pulled right up to where we were camped, parked, and three soldiers with automatic weapons jumped out of their vehicles.

The soldiers were faced with three people lying on mats on the ground eating energy bars – not a particularly threatening sight, but still they had a job to do, and we were it. They were talking quickly in Arabic, and we were asking them to slow down. We were saying in Arabic, "Please speak slowly," but they were not really listening. They didn't know what we were doing there, and we were not able to explain. We were trying to explain in French, which was our best chance, then in Arabic, where we didn't have enough vocabulary, but nothing was working.

There we were, trying everything, and it just wasn't working. I was using every reference that I possibly could to let them know that we were harmless, there was no problem here. We tried to convey to them that we'd go back to town if we had to, and even though the military base was just over the hill and we could see down into it, we weren't spying.

After running through probably a dozen different ideas, my next idea was, Muhammad Ali, the boxer. I announced, I know Muhammad Ali, which of course I don't. I know a little about boxing, maybe even a lot about boxing, but I certainly didn't personally know Muhammad Ali.

That changed everything. It really changed everything. They became friendly, put their guns away, and sat down. All they wanted to know was, "What's he like?" They let out some French they knew, and we talked a little

French with them. Everything became friendly. What we eventually found out, was that the taxi driver who dropped us off went back to town, and told the military exactly where we were so he wouldn't get in trouble. They always knew. We were never a secret. Eventually they gave us a ride back into town and told us the best way to get on the plane the next day. We did get on the plane the next day, but that's another story that I'm not going to tell now.

My 11th language, my 11th frame of reference, was what made me able to communicate something of good will to these soldiers. They were able to feel something of friendliness, something of common interest, and that we were no danger to them.

Right then I confirmed something that I had long suspected. I verified that knowing how to communicate with people doesn't only mean knowing a lot of words in your own language, or even in foreign languages (though that skill can certainly help). It means having varied experiences in life, and being able to recognize that people have varied experiences in life, and being able to talk to people with the frame of reference of those varied experiences. On the plane the next day, as it was flying us straight to Tamanrasset, we talked enthusiastically of our realizations about communication. We talked about that same subject when we rendezvoused with our friends in the Hogar Mountains in the far south of the Algerian Sahara.

I have made those skills part of my program, and many people I know have also seen fit to make it part of their program. If you want to really be able to share what you understand with others, especially when it's not for your benefit, but for theirs, you have to have varied life experiences. So if people lack experience in their exposure to nature, they should get that experience. If people lack experience in their exposure to business and monetary matters, they should get that experience. Playing music, building houses, driving a stick shift, cooking food – all of those languages, all those frames of reference are important for a person who aspires to communicate. The book you are reading is an example of this different kind of multilinguality.

Yes, the words are in the English language, but the meanings are in the languages of the multifaceted nature of human life.

Chapter 3
Swindled

I heard on the news that something called an eclipse is going to happen today around 6 pm. I want to take the gift of that news report to explain scientifically, something which you might not have realized. There is really no such thing as an eclipse. Nothing is really happening, other than we happen to be standing in a particular position at which two things appear to be crossing.

There is a rock formation by the highway in Utah called Old Woman Rock. For a few seconds, as you're driving by, from that one vantage point, this rock has that appearance to us. The rest of the time it is what it is. Similarly, if I were to stand up in my seat in a theater, only those behind me would have an obstructed view of the screen. No one else would have that perspective but those behind me. For everyone else nothing is happening. An eclipse is a verb – it's a moving of objects that are constantly in motion. Nothing is happening to the moon and nothing is happening to the sun. Neither of those objects is taking part in the eclipse. The only element that makes this non-event attractive to us is a third element – to us the most important element – and that is us. The eclipse is all about *us*. It's an *us* observation. To make it into anything else, is to make it even more about us.

This temporary point of view, which it most accurately is, does affect our vision in an interesting way because we see a different lighting of our Earth. I was in Alaska in mid-summer some years ago. It gets dark very late there, and you find yourself eating dinner at midnight. Flying in an airplane you can be looking down at the sunset rather than up at it – it's interesting to look down at the clouds. It's a different perspective, an interesting and curious one . . . but nothing is happening.

Nothing is happening except your perspective is from a particular place. Your point of view is from a particular place. It's all about our point of view – not a phenomenon of the sun or the moon. They're doing what they always do.

Bob Dylan sings, *We've been fooled into thinking the finishing end is at hand*. We read about something on the Web. We hear people talk about it on TV. It's become an event, and we become interested in that event. Is anything actually happening, or is it only the point from which we are viewing – our point of view?

I'm not changing the subject by asking you if you're familiar with the name Harry Marcopoulos. He was a financial investigator, and the first person to have an inkling that there was some kind of financial swindling going on with Bernie Madoff and his empire. Madoff spent years masterminding a pyramid scheme, where individuals, organizations, and retirement funds were putting millions and millions of dollars into his investment fund. It actually was a pyramid scheme – one in which people would eventually be losing all their money.

Harry Marcopoulos worked as a fraud investigator for the U.S. Securities and Exchange Commission. He suspected Madoff, but couldn't get anyone to listen to him. He pursued this investigation for ten years – sometimes for agencies, and a lot of the time on his own. He had very little success in getting attention, until Bernie Madoff's financial empire started to disintegrate, and people started tangibly losing money. It must have been a very frustrating experience for Harry Marcopoulos.

Our lives have become part of a pyramid scheme – a swindle. What we're seeking comes from a point of view that has been presented to us as fact. There are no eclipses and there is no, as Leonard Cohen says, *card that is so high and wild we'll never need to deal another.* I'm concerned about the global deception of what success is, and what fulfillment is. I'm concerned that we've been swindled into a distorted understanding as to what it means to be happy, and how one goes about that. I'm concerned that we've become convinced that our misfortunes are real, and not caused simply because of the point from which we're viewing them – our point of view.

We imagine that our lives have been eclipsed, and that this eclipsing is an actuality. We have fallen victim to our own unique pyramid scheme – not one caused by the greed of Bernie Madoff. We are victims of having been convinced that the actions we're taking to get recognition, to get approval, to become wealthy, to feel insulated, to be supported by reputation, are going to lead us to happiness and contentment. We are victims of the story that there is some deep and meaningful reward to accomplishment, and that there is some deep and meaningful reward to having other people think that we're wonderful. If enough people say we're wonderful, we may actually be wonderful.

Yes, there is a deeply meaningful reward and experience in human life, but it doesn't come from those things. Sure it's nice to be comfortable, have leisure, and be in control. But that comfort, leisure, and control are only what we're after on the surface of things. What we're really after is something more than that. We have been swindled by the fraudulent promise that there is a peaceful resting place that we can get to by being recognized, by having a list of people that can give testimony to our accomplishments. We have come to believe that we will feel good because of their testimony, and we will be insulated from the wounds that life can deal.

I feel like Harry Marcopoulos – that somebody has to make a statement – someone has to explain that this is not the case; there is fraud going on here. No, not malevolent fraud, but the unconscious spreading of the false conclusion that an eclipse is more than a point of view, and your troubles are more than a point of view. If you hadn't bought that story, you would know that your solutions are distorted ones, because those solutions are meant to solve actualities – and most of your troubles are not actualities. Your troubles are only impediments to achieving something that wouldn't bring you what you really want anyway.

The actuality is, that we have human lives, and those lives carry with them a promise. It's not a religious promise, it's not a spiritual promise, it's a natural promise that we've been given. We can actually rediscover our connection to the energy that keeps it all going – to the energy that keeps us alive. I'm not referring to a religious experience, but the natural experience that people have moved so far away from.

Chapter 4
At The Zoo

I want to say a few things about the 2016 Olympics that went on recently in South America, and on TV everywhere. Not so much because it was a recent craze or infatuation, or because it was what was happening and a popular subject then, but more because I might have a perspective about that particular phenomenon that you might find interesting – one that might reflect on something that could be a reason why we're sharing words together right now.

As I was watching the gymnastics competition, I realized that something about it looked familiar. I was watching these young girls on the uneven parallel bars swinging, swinging, swinging, and I knew I'd seen that before somewhere other than in gymnastics competition. At first I couldn't remember where I'd seen it, but then I remembered where. It was at the zoo. Traveling to numerous foreign countries avails a person to many zoo-visiting opportunities, so I've been to a lot of zoos. You can learn things about a society by seeing how they take care of their animals.

In one of those countries, I must have seen a zoo with something akin to uneven parallel bars, and seen chimpanzees or gibbons or some kind of ape swinging similarly on them, with at least the level of proficiency of humans, no matter how proficient they have become.

I didn't think much about it until later when I was watching the swimming races. I found them extraordinary to watch, especially since I'm somewhat of a swimmer and have been all my life. When the swimmers start off the race, or come off the wall on a flip turn, they do a very graceful undulating kick for a few yards known as the dolphin kick. As I was watching the racers, I knew that I had also seen *that* before somewhere. This time I remembered immediately where I'd seen it – at the aquarium. Every fish in creation does that kick. Not only dolphins do that kick, but all fish do that kick – also as easily and proficiently as our most competent swimmer.

So I put these two observations together, and realized that what we're doing in our quest for excellence, is we're competing with animals. We're applauding our hard-earned success at being able to run half as fast as an animal, and jump half as high as another one. We're competing with the capacities that animals have – ones in which they naturally excel. In being so enamored with our success in our quest to imitate animals, we have completely ignored the quest for excellence in the capacity that humans have that animals don't.

Fifty million people worldwide are not watching us display our intellectual and emotional attempts at excellence are they? We're not trying to achieve brilliance in those areas – brilliance of emotion, brilliance of thought. We have no

Olympics for those things, certainly not that have proliferated to the degree the physical ones have. Yes, we are physical animals like they are, but is that all we are? Should our most celebrated undertakings be to imitate *their* physical attributes? No human being can run as fast as an animal. No human being can jump as high as an animal. No human being can do the acrobatics of an animal. Animals already demonstrate the manifestation of excellence in those areas. Why are we putting so much energy into the attaining of excellence in those capacities, while attaining excellence in our unique capacities is being left by the wayside?

We are also imitating animals in the way we go about displaying these physical attainments of ours. The entire Olympic event, and other events like it, are based on the necessity for competition with each other to demonstrate excellence – which is another animal trait.

Competition is a necessity in the animal world, or the animal kingdom as we call it. Competition for food, competition for territory, competition for propagational rights to guarantee survival of the species, are all natural elements of life for animals in the wild. Animals have to compete with each other. Human beings don't have to compete with each other! Yes, we have learned from our predecessors that competition is a necessity in all phases of human life, but it is definitely not. The basis of excellence in this extremely popular, extremely magnetic event is imitating animals in their capacity – trying to get as good as they are, and using competition with each other, to both achieve and demonstrate that imitation.

At one time I was a relatively dedicated horse rider. In my late teenage years, I breezed horses at the race track, and later, as an adult I owned horses. I wasn't a jockey, but I was an exercise boy, and as an exercise boy I did what were called *speed runs*. In order to get a horse to run its fastest time, we would get a pace horse to run along with it – a horse with early speed to get it going in the beginning, and a horse with closing speed to get it running its fastest at the end – horses running along with it the whole time – sound familiar? A horse doesn't have available to it the concept of doing its best. It needs competition to excel.

That is the nature of competition in the Olympics. People do their best because they're being pushed through competition with each other. We're using imitation of physical attributes of animals, and we're isolating those capacities and combining them with another animal capacity, competition, to create an event that the whole world is watching and participating in – an event like no other.

It is only *between* people that competition is a distortion. When we compete with ourselves to become better humans, great results can be achieved. Whether we would care to acknowledge it or not, we are in competition with nature, and that competition is actual, not a self-generated distortion like the competition between people. When there are natural disasters – phenomena of nature – those events frequently facilitate people to rise to occasions of humanity that are rarely seen otherwise.

I have personally witnessed the working together that happens when nature upsets the plans of humans. Several years ago a number of my friends and I traveled to the town of Pearlington, Mississippi – a place that was devastated by the winds and water provoked by Hurricane Katrina. Our aim was to spend a month lending assistance, through both our construction skills and our financial contributions. The scene there was one of intense cooperation between civic groups, religious groups, black people, white people, residents, visitors, volunteers, and professional relief workers. Everyone worked together, ate together, and solved problems together. This extremely human result was precipitated by our competition with nature, not our competition with each other.

We are perpetually confronted with our competition with nature not only through natural disasters but in more frequent examples. The world population has grown geometrically in the last 100 years, and the need for research and development in food production has never been so important. Nature is not always so generous with its rainfall, and growing food depends on rainfall. Yes, there are companies that provide that service, but they are motivated by financial profit – they compete with each other for markets and products. They are not competing with nature and its fickle rainfall.

Drug companies could be competing with nature for the discovery of medicines that would cure disease and alleviate suffering. This competition has the potential of being an example of the type of competition that facilitates working together, but it doesn’t go that way. Human greed, an artificial component brought on by fear, enters the formula. These companies are no longer competing with nature for cures, but competing with each other for markets and profits. Had they actually been competing for cures, they would have found their companies working together, rather than against each other.

Understanding the diabolical and often confusing subject of competition can cause us to wonder about the gravity of the message put forth by the Olympics: people can get together over imitating animals through competition with each other, and that is the best way we have to transcend our physical differences, racial differences, national differences – that is our hope, our way. What a distortion, what a misleading concept that is.

Muhammed Ali was an incredible athlete – an incredible boxer. But more incredible than his boxing and athletic skill was that he combined his boxing with poetry. He was a boxing poet. Poetry is not one of the capacities of an animal. It is one of the emotional capacities of a human being. He also was a person familiar with violence, in that he was a boxing professional, the heavyweight champion of the world several times. He depended on his fists, and on how hard and how quickly he could hit his opponent. Muhammed Ali refused to fight in the army – an emotional and intellectual decision. People all over the world don't know the names Joe Lewis, Rocky Marciano, Ingemar Johansson, or Floyd Patterson, all heavyweight champions of the world, but they know the name Muhammed Ali – because he was not only a physical champion, but because he also pursued excellence in our uniquely human capacities of intellect and emotion.

Is it really for better health that we pursue yoga, and health food, and exercise? Or is it that we are trying to create some level of perfection with our bodies, because it is a more accessible accomplishment than trying to achieve excellence with our intellect and emotions? The human body has already evolved into the most perfect instrument it will ever be. That has already happened. No torture that a nine-year-old girl can be made to endure, in order to learn some artificial swinging through the trees like a gorilla, is going to make that body any more evolved. The body is done with its evolution. It is true that we're doing things to degrade it, to make it less efficient, through polluted atmosphere, unhealthy food, smoking, and stress. Avoiding these self-destructive elements is certainly worthwhile, but the evolving component of the human experiment is not the body, and will not be the body. No animal-imitated accomplishment fueled by competition with each other will change that, no matter how high we jump, or how fast we run.

So why do we adulate those who undergo torture to make the body do all these things that come naturally to animals? Perhaps we don't realize that in uplifting those accomplishments, we both lose our energy and dampen our enthusiasm for feeding the evolving parts of our humanity – parts which are still in their infancy – our higher intellect and our higher emotions. We do not share these capacities with other animals; they are uniquely human. *They are the growing end of the human race*. Those capacities are not being challenged, tested, or explored, to anywhere near the degree that this other dead end exploration is pursued. All our energy goes into this dead end quest, and very little of our energy goes into the living end.

Chapter 5
The Written Word

The degradation of our valuation for excellence through intellect and emotion is growing and is surfacing in many different facets of our lives. One facet far from athletic competition is the world of books and reading. I came to value reading books long after my schooldays. For years I interpreted reading, as a tool for education, as a burden. Now, as one who has gained great benefit from reading, I've become a big proponent of the potential positive influence of the written word. I've read many books – some over and over again. I've written some, and right now I'm writing one.

As an author, I've recently found it necessary to do some research into the changing environment of publishing that advanced technology has precipitated. Here are some interesting facts: in 1940, there were 4,000 books published. To give you a relative perspective, in the year 2000, 50,000 books were published. Fifty thousand new books went into bookstores in the year 2000 . . . 4,000 in 1940. Amongst those books in 1940 was *For Whom the Bell Tolls* by Ernest Hemingway, Jung's book *Religion and Psychology*, Gandhi's *Experiments in Truth, The Heart is a Lonely Hunter* by Carson McCullers, and *Native Son* by Richard Wright – probably the first book written describing the modern African

American experience. All these incredible books, exploratory books, not books repeating things that were said before, but books exploring relationships that hadn't been explored before, were among the 4,000 books that were published in 1940. In addition to those, the delightful classics, Dumbo and Pinocchio, were both published in 1940.

All those books had a chance to be discovered because they were among 4,000, not 50,000. It's even hard to discover an incredible book amidst 4,000 other books, but it's possible. But then 50,000 books at the turn of this century; how could Hermann Hesse and his masterpieces have been discovered amongst 50,000 books? They would have been lost. A publisher would have said, "That's too long . . . it's too long, and not that many people are interested in the subject." How many people would have discovered the books of Laurens Van der Post amidst 50,000 books, most written in an attempt to make money through publishers also trying to make money?

As a product of my recent research, I have also discovered the latest in the publishing evolution – *On Demand* publishing. The process allows a person to send a PDF of either something they've put together in two weeks, or the contents of their diary, or details of how they've solved their digestive problems, to a printing company, along with a drawing for a cover, and if that printer is equipped with the appropriate technology, they can print one book or five books or 50 books and it will look exactly like a book in a book store. They'll charge you $5-$10 dollars a book to do it, and you'll have your book in a week.

Now I know from my history in publishing, that even 10 years ago to get 1,000 books printed would have cost a lot more than $5 per book. In order for the cost to be low enough to make a profit, a reasonable run for a publisher would have been an order of 20,000 books, and the waiting time for that order would have been six months. If you wanted to have your own book printed, so you could give it away to family and friends, it would have been impossible to find a book printer that would have wasted his time with such a small order, or else it would have cost you $200 per book. How could they do it for less? They would have had to set it up on a press, and do the whole process like they were printing and binding 20,000 books. You would probably have been advised, "Go to Kinko's, make photo copies, and have them put the pages together with rings and you'll have something nice for yourself, because we can't do it."

That's something I know about publishing, so when I discovered in my recent research that you can get a professionally produced book in a week for a few dollars, I thought, *that is impossible*. Hey, that's not even the whole story! Not only will they make that professional quality book for you, but they'll put your book on Amazon, and if one gets ordered they will print that one as needed, ship it to the customer, and give you some money as a royalty payment.

These claims sounded absurd to me until my Googling brought me to the discovery that there is now a machine which a PDF on your computer or thumb drive can be plugged into – it cuts the papers, prints the cover, wraps and glues it to the pages, and in less than a minute it produces a library-quality paperback, called a perfect-bound paperback. This machine exists in printing companies around the country. So now, with this deal, anyone can get their book printed and for sale on Amazon. They will only have to pay for the number of books they want to give away to their friends and family, because nobody else cares about this book about their digestion. So if you want to do that, you can buy ten books for $7 a book, give them away, and if any more of your books happen to sell on Amazon, which they probably won't, unless you have an uncle somewhere who will order it, they will print one for you and send it to this person, and send you $2 a book or whatever the royalty is for that book.

Now it is 2016, and the 50,000 books published in the year 2000 when it would be impossible to find Herman Hesse or Laurens Van der Post and others and others and others, have grown to one million – one million books (including this one). How can a hidden gem be found amongst one million books? It can't. I'm telling you this really sad story about the end of books, because the valuation for the exploration of the intellect and the emotions that is created in one book out of 1,000 books, is now not going to be accessible, because out of one million books, how can you find that current *For whom the Bell Tolls* or *Native Son* or *Heart of the Lonely Hunter,* or even *Dumbo*? You can't.

Spiritual enlightenment is a product of the expansion of ordinary intellect into higher and finer intellect and eventually beyond; of ordinary emotion to higher and finer emotion and eventually beyond. It is the natural evolution of human expansion – the natural evolution of human growth from its growth end – its intellect and emotion.

When human intellect is unrestricted, it has the unique potential to think creatively without imitation – to conceive of almost anything. Human intellect can do so much more than memorize. *Jeopardy* – the longest running show on television, is a game that only challenges the intellect's ability to memorize; it doesn't challenge the ability to create and combine things that have not been combined before – like poetry and boxing, like music and nature. The intellect has so much more expanded potential. That is the growing part of the human race.

Similarly, human emotion has so much more potential than, "I like, I don't like, this feels good, this doesn't feel good, I'm afraid, I'm anxious, I'm relaxed, I'm up-tight." We can actually feel, not feel with our bodies, but feel the nature of life with our emotional ability. We can feel not only personal love, but that fineness that love represents in relation to everything outside and inside ourselves. That is within the human capacity, that is the human growing end, and the natural evolution of that growth is spiritual. Spirituality is not a separate quest. A path is not spiritual because it talks about spiritual subjects. There are no spiritual subjects. There are human beings and uncharted territory, and that is the territory of the higher intellect and of the higher emotions. The only way to explore that uncharted territory is to leave some of the obstacles and restrictions behind.

If a person learns to leave the fear behind that constricts emotions, if a person learns to leave the embarrassment of loss of self-image behind, and the timidity and carefulness that cloak our finer emotional capacity behind, then they can expand into what human beings are capable of . . . and without competition with each other.

The intellect is flooded with unexamined concepts. *That's good, that's right, that's the way it's done* – driving us into imitating what happened before. No creativity. In the big band era, musicians sat on chairs with music stands in front of them. All the big bands did that. Someone was first, but all that followed were imitators. Years later that was replaced by four guys in suits standing on a stage – three in the front and a drummer behind. (Yes, the Beatles and the Rolling Stones started out in suits.) Every band that followed, copied that model, until musicians began to wear street clothes when they performed, and then every band copied *that* model – all imitation. Now, singers run back and forth on the stage and think they are 100% original, because they're running back and forth on the stage wearing a baseball hat, which is the current country and western running up and down the stage, rather than running up and down the stage with a cowboy hat. It's all imitation; there's no creativity there.

We're not exploring our human capacity when we have restrictions that say this is the way it's done, or when we're following by doing what we're told without questioning. Because there is no way it's done; there's a way it used to be done. Creativity is thinking, "If I were to build it right now, if I were to set it up right now, with everything I know, everything I understand, everything I've seen, how would *I* set it up?" Not, "How did *they* set it up?" but, "How would *I* set it up?"

This lack of originality, this imitation, is not limited to any one aspect of our lives. It is pervasive, and finds its way into behavioral subtleties in the way we talk to each other, the way we furnish our houses, and the choices of clothes that we wear. The unspoken mantra being, *How is it done? What are the rules here*? Would our actions have to look entirely different? Not necessarily . . . but they would be a product of original thought – not copying. Those actions would be part of the growing end of the human race.

Without examining hundreds of unexamined concepts, very few of which you are aware, how could you possibly move on to a place of freedom to think and feel originally? How could you possibly move on to finer emotions, with the restriction of the negative emotions – minute embarrassments, and anxieties which you have in numbers that you would certainly underestimate? Until you leave them behind, how could you possibly move on to the exploration of the capacity of emotion? You couldn't.

Some state-of-the-art exploration of the obstacles and resistance to this quest of expanding emotions and intellect is going to be necessary, and that's only for the resistance part. Once the resistance is removed, or removes itself, or is left behind, then there's the exploration. Then you can actually ask questions. You can see something and think something that nobody else thought before, or have a feeling for something that nobody else felt before. You actually can do that. Now, all you can do is take a little bit of yourself and add it to everything you imitate. You can imagine that you're an original because there's a little of you in it. Real attainment isn't competing with the achievements of animals. There is actually a unique human possibility.

How could a school be a spiritual school if it didn't help a person move in the direction of becoming an unrestricted human being – a human being free from the restrictions of negative emotions, and the restrictions and limitations of unexamined concepts? Meditation may be the ultimate exercise of a spiritual school, but it is for human beings, not for entities that imitate animals and other humans, and only do their best when competition with each other is available.

Chapter 6
Bethany

I can recall the extremely high academic pressure of the time when I was a teenager. This was especially prevalent in my last couple of years of high school. It was the time to make a decision about what I was going to do after graduation. In the environment in which I lived, it was not so much a decision of what I would do after high school, but what college I would go to. Most of the kids I hung out with were much more directed than I, being destined for doctor and lawyer-hood. At the time, I was extremely purposeless academically, and didn't feel destined for anything in particular. For me, and the rest of us that weren't on such a clear track, it was a notably difficult time. About six months before graduation, representatives from our high school newspaper came around to all the seniors, and asked for a blurb about what we were going to do after we got out of school.

Of course, all of my friends already knew what they were going to do. The closest I had come to even applying to college was a few inquiries through some relatives that were either on the board of directors, or alumni of certain colleges. These relatives were calling me and saying, "I know your grades aren't that great, and I know you're not that motivated, but I'll say a few words for you and help get you into my school."

In the back of my mind, I figured that I could fall back on that, but I hadn't even sent in an application at that point. Of course, I felt I had to give some response to the school newspaper. So I just made up having been admitted to one of the schools connected to my relatives and told the reporter that's where I was going. As time proceeded, I heard the words fairly frequently from my mother, "Well, what are you going to do? Where are you going to go?" It was getting into summer, past the time that it was realistically possible to apply, and all I had done was go to a couple of interviews. I could tell you long stories about some of the interviews that I went to – ones that my relatives arranged. One thing was for sure, those interviews were definitely an embarrassment to each of the relatives that had arranged them.

I remember an interview at Brandeis University, a college with very high academic standards. I had an uncle on the board of directors who arranged the interview. I remember the interviewer asking, "So, what kind of books do you read?" At that point all I read were horseracing forms. That's what I read. That was my reading, those racing charts. "Oh," I said, "I read poetry." So he asked, "Which poets do you read?" I hadn't prepared anything, because I really wasn't even motivated to do that. All I could think of were poems from English class. So I said,

"Well, I guess I don't read that much poetry." And that was one of my better interviews – so you get the picture.

Summer was almost over and I still had no place to go. About that time I started considering another option. I had a friend who came from a religious Christian family. My family didn't have any strong religious affiliation – and if it had one, it probably wouldn't have been Christian. I guess it was basically random. I had three different religions represented in my family. After they got through battling about which one I should follow, everybody decided to give up the whole thing, so there wasn't much of anything there for me religion-wise.

A friend of mine, Neil, was going to a small (600 students) Disciples of Christ College in West Virginia. So I figured maybe I'd go with Neil. I phoned the school and found out that it was very easy to get in. I wrote a letter telling them that I wanted to attend. They got my grades, which were somewhere in the middle, my SAT tests, which were a little better than that, my tuition money, which was probably the clincher, and in two weeks I was admitted.

The school was virtually in the middle of hillbilly-dirt-floor-shack nowhere. I was used to a much higher amount of stimulation around me, so instead of going to class, I spent most of my time trying to work out where I was going to go for entertainment, and how I was going to keep busy when I wasn't studying – which was always. There were a few other freshman from big cities, some more restless than others, and one of the ways we kept busy was going to town.

Town was Wheeling, which was about a 40-minute drive away on local roads through the West Virginia mountains. I remember a time in November (I only lasted until Christmas) when I was pacing the floors of the dormitory. It was getting to be evening and it was snowing out. I had a car there, but to drive someplace in the snow would have been reckless. I was really restless, so I tried to get other kids to go to Wheeling with me, but I couldn't. It was even more of a confrontation because I had to go by myself, but since I couldn’t sit still, I got in the car and did this stupid thing – I drove into Wheeling.

It was a midweek night and there was a weekly dance at the nursing school there. Kids from our school often drove in, though certainly not on this night – but I did, and I was the only one. I remember going in and seeing nursing students there and other people too. If you are a guy alone, you ask girls to dance; there’s nothing else to do. If I had known people there, I could have hung out and talked, but I didn’t, so I asked this girl to dance – her name was Betty. We were dancing and she asked, "You come from Bethany, don't you?" and I said, "Yeah." We were trading small talk, and I was trying to be cool of course, because a young guy in that situation is trying to be cool. After a few minutes she said to me, "You don't have to play it cool with me. I know that if you came all the way over here from Bethany in this weather, you must be desperate."

Hearing those words from a stranger you’re dancing with is not the kind of thing a young man forgets. One does not remember something from that far back unless it was significant, and the significance to me was that she was straight with me. I knew that I needed the activity, I needed the content, and I wanted some company, so with that aside, we could proceed. We didn’t have to deal with the bullshit.

So instead of finding a lover that didn't blow my cover, I found an aspiring nun that blew my cover.

Do you know why I'm telling you this story? Because if you're still reading this book, I know you must want something. We can get that out of the way. You aren't writing a review for the local newspaper, you aren't just passing the time. You really want something. I know that about you. People wouldn't read this book past the first couple of chapters if they didn't really want something. Wouldn't that be really wonderful if we didn't have to deal with the bullshit? Think of how often in life we have to deal with bullshit. Maybe we don't have to deal with the bullshit in this situation, because I know you really want something, and you have not found it, because otherwise you wouldn't be still reading this – you'd be with John Grisham.

You may not be desperate, but you really want something. You've had a flash somewhere, an experience somewhere, and those experiences have told you that repetition of what you've done before will not deliver what you suspect is possible. So you're back on the road as a seeker, which is a really wonderfully opened-door place. So I want to start off by telling you a little bit about possibilities as I see them, now that we have gotten the first part out of the way.

Chapter 7
Amazing Grace

So . . . there I was, at Bethany College, in a little town about fifty miles from Wheeling, West Virginia. If any of you are alumni of that college, I congratulate you on what I assume was your eventual escape. Needless to say, it was very disorienting for me. Not only was it rural, but it was very provincial, and I was from the Big Apple.

Freshman didn't have any choice of classes. At some schools the students have choices, but not at Bethany. One of the courses I was assigned was a religious studies type bible class. It was my first class of the morning and it started at 7:30 am. All the freshman lived in dormitories, so we would just walk over – you know, get up at 7:28, be in bible class at 7:30. Having zero interest even in my favorite course at Bethany, and certainly a lot less than that in bible class, made mornings not my favorite time.

After taking attendance, the first thing we did every morning was to stand up and sing *Amazing Grace*. That was a hellish experience for me. I could just as well have been singing the Star Spangled Banner – or what I phoneticized at the age of six as the Star Scrambled Banana. I could have been singing anything. It was really meaningless to me. Still, every morning I stood up and sang that song. Consistent with the rest of the rules of this particular college, was the one that required us to sit in assigned seats. Diabolically, I was a "G" – for my last name, Gold, so I sat in the front row. I guess there weren't many early letters represented, because I had nobody in front of me to hide behind, so I actually had to sing the song.

Every day I started my day with *Amazing Grace,* so I know the words to that song. It eventually came to pass, not at that time, but much later – actually years and years later, that this particular song, *Amazing Grace*, was reintroduced to me. The words had continued to be familiar, but the meaning became significant for me as well – a meaning that had never been of consequence before. To this day, I think that the combination of my original lack of recognition for the meaning of the words to this song, juxtaposed to my eventual realization, recognition, and experience of what this song means, has brought *Amazing Grace* into the position of probably being the most meaningful song there is to me.

Amazing Grace, how sweet the sound
That saved a wretch like me.
I once was lost but now I'm found
Was blind but now I see.
'Twas Grace that taught my heart to feel
And Grace my fears released.
Most precious day when Grace appeared
The hour I first believed.

I know that everybody has heard these words before, and probably for some of you there is a degree of experience connected with them that is considerably deeper than my experience was at Bethany College, outside of Wheeling, West Virginia. This Grace, this Amazing Grace, that appears in the hour when we first believe, has been attributed to Christianity, or a religious belief, or a doctrine or a dogma, but my frame of reference was probably more scientific than any of these. Whatever the context from which our concept of those words comes, there is an experience, there is a tangibility, there is even a materiality of this force that we call Grace – one that is usually understood as something assembled from completely emotional ingredients.

Defining Grace as an emotional, religious element is too limiting though, because Grace is a magnetic force that actually has a tangibility that we know very little about. It has an indispensable function that we must learn to appreciate, because this force that we call Grace, which people think of as something esoteric, ephemeral, and intangible, happens to be a critically elemental factor in the formula for becoming a good person in actuality, a transcendent person in actuality, and an enlightened person in actuality. So whatever we do or have done to improve ourselves, whatever we've done to reach for something higher, if that indispensable tangible element of Grace has not been included, we may imagine that things have transpired, but in actuality, nothing new has occurred.

It's similar to going on a camping trip and taking some of that powdered stuff along that's called dehydrated soup. If you don't have water, or you don't eventually get water – you will never have soup. If you pass a cup of that powder to somebody with a soup spoon and say, "Here, have some," they'll look at it and they won't see any soup there, and there won't *be* any soup there, because there is no soup without water. So as water is to soup, Grace is to all our goals of consciousness. All aspirations to transcend the ordinariness of life, the heaviness of life, the lack of perspective of life, everything that we've done to realize that we're part of a creation, that we're part of something bigger – all the awakened soup that we've tried to make of ourselves, without this water that is Grace, it won't and can't happen.

If we temporarily agree to accept this hypothesis, it's interesting where that agreement will take us. It would mean that whatever books we read, whatever methods we use, whatever people we hook up with, whatever systems we participate in, whatever we take on, we're going to need that *something* that has been, up to now, invisible to us. We must add that ingredient, which is actually a force, to the other ingredients which are more obvious to us.

So what do we know about petitioning this force of Grace, this upward motion of the energy of creation that is constantly but impersonally beckoning its components (us) to return to it, and consistently standing in opposition to the forces that repel – the ones that manifest as obstacles to our freedom? What do we know about this force that originates from the energy that keeps everything together, and gives breath to the totality, and in doing so, feeds breath to our individuality?

Simply stated – whatever we know or don't know about Grace – we need to get it on our side. Or better stated: How are we going to get on its side? Can we bribe it? What is its monetary system? Can we cajole it? Can we convince it? Where are its weak points? How can we flatter it? How can we con it? We want to bring into play all the methods of seduction in which we've become skilled. And those of us who have tried all those methods (because those, of course, are the first ones that we try), find that they don't work.

It's like trying to exchange coins in a foreign country. You can exchange dollar bills in almost any foreign country, but when you bring out your coins they say, "No thanks." It may be that a hundred quarters make $25, but in a foreign country, a hundred quarters don't make $25. Our accustomed methods of interacting don't work when it comes to petitioning Grace. So what is the system of interaction between this force of Grace and these components of individuality, the ones that we call "me"?

We have become victims of a term whose meaning has been highly distorted. When we think that we have to be religious to embrace this concept, we are mistaken. The only thing that this natural force has to do with any religion, is that Grace has created the essence of each religion.

Chapter 8
The Russian Host

My ancestors came from Russia, but until recently it had been one of the few countries in the world that I hadn't visited. Had I known in advance the complexity of the procedure for Americans to get a tourist visa to Russia, I actually might not have gone. We had to fill out numerous documents and give references both here and there, in addition to producing evidence that we had places to stay – besides which the visa is inordinately expensive compared to anyplace else in the world. We were halfway through this procedure before we realized all this, and you know how it goes – once you're halfway through something you probably wouldn't have done had you known what you know now – you're probably going to finish it anyway – and we did.

Last spring several friends and I went to Russia. We decided that the best way to enter the country was through Estonia, a small country on its northwest border. Estonia is a Baltic Sea country just north of two other Eastern European countries, Latvia and Lithuania. We thought it would be interesting to spend a little time in Estonia, since it has an interesting past and an even more interesting present, in addition to a nice sounding second syllable. So we flew from San Francisco to England, and from England to Estonia, and were glad we did.

The country is known for its people singing together. People there have numerous national and private choirs and frequently get together to sing. To find a country where the people have a lot of national pride of a nice kind is extremely refreshing. On our last night in Tallinn, the capital city, we went to a singing fest at the university, where 20,000 people of all ages were singing folk songs together. It was quite a sight and sound experience. Our intention was to spend a week in Estonia, and from there take a train across the border to St. Petersburg – a six or seven-hour train ride.

The last night in our guest house was spent figuring out our logistics for the coming days. We still didn't know how we were going to get from the train station to a car rental place; we needed a car because we wanted to go to more remote places in Russia than a person generally goes to – not just Moscow and St. Petersburg. All our logistics were indefinite, because all the information on Russian websites was in the Russian language, written in the Cyrillic alphabet. We knew *da* and *nyet,* and quite a few more words and phrases, but we couldn't decipher the websites. There was no way. We couldn't do it.

Fortunately, there was a very friendly English-speaking Russian lady who was also staying at our guesthouse. She helped us figure out all our planes, trains, and automobiles from about 9 or 10 at night until 1 or 2 in the morning. She really hung in there with us. Russian travel information is not what it is in most other parts of the world. We thanked her, and she gave us her name and phone number in Moscow.

Later that morning, she left for wherever she was going, and we left to take the train from Tallinn across the border to St. Petersburg, which turned out to be a really wonderful train ride. We spent a few days in St. Petersburg, and eventually got a car and drove through some extremely remote areas that were the highlight of traveling in Russia for me. Once you get away from the cities, the villages and the roads that connect them become surprisingly primitive for such an advanced country.

We ended up in Moscow where we returned our car, did some sightseeing, and proceeded to look up someone whose name we were given before we left the U.S. This person was supposed to have some connection to Sufism, or some spiritual group. When you're in a foreign country, it's always nice to know somebody who lives there; without local contacts one can rarely see the insides of life. We phoned this guy, Sergei, and he told us that he would love to get together with us. We were staying at a local hostel, and he suggested he come there to pick us up and take us out somewhere. We figured to first spend a while in the hostel living room with him – maybe play some music before we went wherever. We had a few musical instruments that we carried with us – a guitar, a flute, a harmonica, a few shakers, all instruments that one or another of us were moderately proficient at playing.

Back in a small town in Estonia, we showed up at a bar with our instruments and played and sang. It was a musical disaster, and was only tolerated because the bartender announced that we were from California – always a curiosity for people who have only heard about the place where movies are made, and a muscle-bound actor had been the governor.

Before we left from the U.S., I was asked a few times, "How come you're going to Russia?" Other than it being a country I've never been to before, I didn't really have a reason. I didn't have something I could say that the person asking would respond to with, "Oh, I see, I understand."

So one of my early aims when we started out, was to come up with a reason, so that when people asked me, "How come Russia?" I could answer. One day on route, we were talking about the term *Oriental*, which is now supposedly politically incorrect to use in reference to a person's ethnicity. People who were Oriental are no longer Oriental – they're Asian. Right then I came up with the reason I was going to Russia, because Russia is one of those countries that is in both Europe and Asia. Russia has a very strong Oriental element to it, or Asian element.

So my reason became, that I was going to study this question. A pursuit which I forgot shortly after arriving, but at least if, *what was I doing there* came up, I had an answer. I was studying the actuality of this politically correctness, and if it indeed existed in Asia. Did people who lived there prefer to be called Asians, or did they maybe even resent not being called Orientals anymore? Maybe this politically correct thing was only something that we invented as proper and was exclusive to us – like you should know that Kundalini isn't pasta. That's enough of that wisecracking – back to my story.

Three people showed up at our Moscow hostel at around 6 pm – Sergei, a middle-aged man with his son, and another man – a close friend. After the necessary greetings, we asked them to hang with us for a while before we all went out. We figured we'd play some music together to break the ice of formality. Even if you have no musical talent, anyone can hit a tambourine, or shake a shaker, or play a drum if they can't play a piano or a guitar. Playing music together has always been part of our dynamic, and I think a really beautiful part. It's not something we were proposing to do as a performance, but something that we could do together for a while to get to know each other.

Hostels usually have a central room with couches, and as they entered, we were sitting in one of those rooms playing and singing. They came and sat with us, but didn't quite know what they were part of. Were we performing for them? What was going on? We did that for a very short while, until it became obvious that they couldn't get into it. Sergei's plan was to go out to a tea/coffee bar, and it seemed like it was time to follow, not lead.

He took us on a long walk around a clubby Moscow neighborhood before we ended up in a dark, narrow, ornately decorated cellar room with twenty or so people lining the walls. He was clearly trying to be the host, and within a few minutes after we sat down, it was easy to see that he was trying too hard. He had such a strong concept that he was going to have to take care of us, that he didn't notice that we didn't need to be taken care of. We certainly didn't need to be taken care of to the degree that he was trying to take care of us. We were supposed to be enjoying ourselves, but he was both unable to relax and having a miserable time.

Everyone probably has, at some time, had that experience, and he was having it then. He was unable to be whoever he was, so we never found out who he was, because he was playing the part of the host the entire time. He was buying us sweets and sweets and sweets . . . how many sweets can you eat? We told him that we were fine and he could sit with us. We asked him questions, but it didn't help, so we spent the time talking to his friend and his son. The boy was a fascinating person. He was twenty years old and had created a website that was extraordinarily popular and prolific in Russia. We had heard that his father was part of a Sufi spiritual organization, and we thought maybe we'd have some common ground to talk about and see what he was into. That never happened. We never got to find out.

When we walked back to the hostel and invited him in to hang around – a situation where he wouldn't have to be the host – he declined. He said they had to go . . . and left, so we never really did have a chance to get to know this person.

This exhaustion that he felt is one that everyone should be familiar with – the exhaustion of putting on a performance, of putting forth something that you imagine is expected, of putting forth your concepts of what's correct behavior for the situation, as opposed to being who you really are in that situation. There is a Jewel song, *Life Uncommon*; the words are, *We are tired, we are weary but we're not worn out*.

Those are the lyrics from a song about freedom. If you're so tired and weary that you're worn out, you're not going to make any more attempts to get free, you're not going to make any attempts to get what's possible, or to get untired or unweary. But if you're not worn out, but only tired and weary – as we all must come to acknowledge that we are – then it's not a depressing realization. It would only be depressing if there was no hope. But if there was hope, it would be an uplifting message to recognize that you're tired and weary of the repetition of your life, of pretending you're someone that you're not.

You're hugging people that you barely know because that's what's done. How do you relate to the people you *really* know? Maybe you have a concept of yourself as friendly or kind, but the kindness is really more your performance than your experience, because you're in need. You're in need like this Russian man was in need. He was trying to fill his need by giving to us, and because it was a performance, it made him tired and weary – I don't know if he was worn out. It's not a pleasant recognition to have about oneself, and it will never happen if you are surrounded by people who are supporting the illusion that everything is okay – because it's not!

If you're thinking, "How could he be so dense as not to see what was going on with himself?" I suspect that you are overestimating people's capacity to see things as they are, when the *they* that is involved is themselves. My neighbor in Arkansas, Claude, was one of those people, as I suspect are many of the rest of our species.

A few words about Claude are probably in order here. Not being able to budget my time adequately in order to write, caused me to choose to spend two plus years at the end of a long gravel road in the Ozark Mountains of Arkansas, where I could work undisturbed to produce words for my first book, *Another Heart in His Hand.* I did, however, go to the town of Batesville once a week for groceries, and on returning to my isolation this particular day, I passed a few guys field burning.

It was a very dry day, of a very dry week, so I stopped and asked what they were up to. They said they had a permit, and the local fire truck was parked nearby. The truck looked like it had been a prop in a Laurel and Hardy movie. I went on to my house and thought about the situation more after I arrived home. I was watching for smoke coming from the direction of the fire, and when it seemed to be increasing, I jumped back in my car and rode the mile back to the fire. It was burning out of control – shooting up the pine trees and bushes, burning everywhere. The wind was also blowing toward my house, so I rushed home, got on the phone, and called the fire department in the nearest town. They made little of it, informing me that there was a local unit on duty there. This *local unit* was a little toot-toot fire truck, and an old guy to match who took care of it. Claude and his fire truck were a matching set.

I wasn't getting anywhere on the phone, so I got back in my Volkswagen bug and drove back to the fire, and parked what I thought would be a safe distance away. The flames were shooting all over the place in front of me, and Claude and the fire truck were parked right in the middle. I shouted to him, asking if there were any other units coming, and he said that he had it all under control. He asked me to help him with the hose. He told me to grab the hose and run with it, because it made the wheel go faster.

As I was running out the length of the hose, I looked back and saw the fire approaching both sides of the fire truck and shooting up in the trees. If you've never seen a forest fire close up (which I hadn't), when it catches on in a sappy tree, it explodes right up the tree. One moment the fire is on the ground, then four seconds later it's 30 feet high and shooting out a lot of heat because of the sap that's burning.

I looked back and saw the fire truck immersed in flames, and the red rotating emergency beacon on top was melting. I shouted, "Claude, the truck!" He heard me, turned around and called back, "No problem, I've got it under control."

It was at that moment that I realized that seeing things as they actually are is not so easy.

Chapter 9
Danner Light Shoes

Yes, we're capable of self-destructive behavior and ignorance, but we're also capable of intuition, inspiration, and compassion. Several years ago, the inhabitants of a village in Africa made that observation about me – and not only about me, but all of us of the materially-developed world. I would not have been a recipient of their wisdom had I not owned a very special pair of boots.

The boots are called Danner Lights. They're wonderful shoes and I've had them for years. When they need new soles, I send them back to the Danner Company and they fix them and send them back to me. That's how much I think of my Danner Lights. They're actually so waterproof that I can walk into water up to my ankles, and when I walk out my feet are still dry.

I got them some years ago before an expedition to North Africa. Toward the end of the expedition I got sick. In remote locations, that can happen, especially if you're not careful. We thought that we were in a place where there were no germs because there were no people, but it wasn't so. We thought we could drink from the occasional sources of water in the middle of the Sahara Desert. As it turned out, though there might not have been cows around, there might have been camels, and even if the camels didn't shit in the water, something always seems to. So you have to put iodine in it – and we hadn't.

At any rate, I got bacterial dysentery. I didn't know at the time what it was, but that's what I got. Sulfur drugs are rarely used anymore in the U.S., so we hadn't brought any with us, so we didn't have the appropriate medicine. I got really sick in the Hogar Mountains of the southern Sahara and spent ten days lying on my back under African skies, looking at the blue of daylight and the black stipple of night. It was a magnificent time for me, even though I was very weak and could barely eat.

Eventually, two of my friends decided they would make the three-day hike into Tamanrasset, the nearest town, to see if they could get medicine. Sure enough, a few days after their departure, a Dutch motorcyclist appeared on a dirt bike bringing us a bottle of sulfur guanidine – which was well known in the area as a sure cure for my malady. I took the medicine and was considerably better the next day. We decided to hike out to the road and wait there for one of the trucks that came by on their way down from the higher mountains. Trucks ran only every few days on that track, and since we didn't know the timing, we just had to get out there and wait – hopefully not for too long. I was very weak. I hiked 100 yards and sat for an hour, and then hiked another

100 yards. Eventually we got to the road and made camp on the side of it. Since it doesn't rain there, we didn't have to set up anything. We just put out our mats and that was camp.

Down the road from where we camped was a village of 100 or so Tuareg tribesmen. We had visited with them, and even spent the night playing music together before we hiked out into the desert. They tried to dissuade us from going into the desert with all kinds of horror stories about what could happen, but we'd run into that before.

Anyway, they spotted us camping by the side of the road and sent a representative from the village to find out what we were doing there. First one visitor, then his wife, then another, then his wife, came out to sit with us. I thought it was their general curiosity, but what they were most fascinated with was my shoes. They just couldn't believe my shoes, my Danner Lights. The message they each took back to their village was, "You've gotta see this guy's shoes." They didn't all come at once, but sooner or later everyone in the village, children and all, made the pilgrimage – and when they arrived they went directly to my shoes.

They spoke a Berber dialect, so our ability to communicate was limited. But some spoke a little French or Arabic, both of which we had a bit of, so we were able to cover the basics. On the day the truck finally came by, I was talking to an older man who had lived in Algeria during the colonial period and spoke pretty good French. He had sat with us often, and I'd made a nice connection with him. I asked him why they were so fascinated with my shoes.

He laughed, and with some embarrassment told me that they were amazed that anybody who could be so stupid as to go out into the most foreboding desert on earth, could come from a country where the people were so smart as to be able to make shoes like those.

The Tuareg were right. Our capacities are so inconsistent. We are capable of doing the absolute craziest, stupidest things – but that's not all we're capable of. We are definitely capable of inspiration and brilliance. Darkness travels through us, hooks us, and pulls us along with it, and light has the capacity to do that as well – an amazing quality of a human being. Our task is very simple. It is to learn to discriminate between the forces that are pulling us – the ones that are pulling us to remember, and the ones that are pulling us to forget, the ones that are pulling us to contract, and the ones that are pulling us to expand.

Chapter 10

The Tiburdans

My ancestors come from Tiburda, a village in the Caucasus Mountains of southern Russia. Small and isolated, Tiburda had existed for hundreds of years on the slopes of Mount Elbrus, the highest mountain in Eastern Europe. A hundred years ago, in that isolated village Muslims, Russian Orthodox Christians, and Jews coexisted, along with a few other ethnic and religious minorities. In those times, religion not only represented the structure of one's theological faith – its ethnic bonds constituted the framework around which people coalesced. But since this village was so isolated, the separations normally expected between Muslim, Jew, and Christian were not as defined. People were unified by necessity against more essential common enemies, which in their case precipitated danger everywhere – especially those incited by nature's rains, floods, and droughts. There were also those fomented by the Cossacks, the legitimate government, and the semi-hostile countries all around them – Tiburda being close to the borders with Turkey and Armenia.

In the early 1900s, as the political situation heated up in anticipation of the First World War, and eventually the Russian revolution, a number of the people in the village decided to leave en masse. The plan was that sixty or seventy men, women, and children would escape over the Caucasus Mountains into Turkey, in an effort to emigrate to the West. The people who were involved in this plan were not necessarily of the same family, or the same ethnic group. Everyone who was willing to make the trip was included. With considerable preparation, they made this arduous journey, and after getting to London, about half continued on to New York.

As you can imagine, an expedition of this kind was so hazardous that the group bonded together even more closely than it had in the village of Tiburda (which no longer exists). When those that continued on from London eventually arrived in New York, all the different families from diverse ethnicities, in order to stick together, cooperatively bought their own apartment house. They recreated their village vertically on Fox Street in the lower East Side of Manhattan, in a neighborhood populated by immigrants from numerous countries and different backgrounds.

In addition to their cooperative living arrangement, and as a method of mutual protection from this new culture that was seeking to assimilate them, they also started several businesses together. The unfamiliarity of the situations in which they found themselves, probably caused them to be fairly closed to those outside of their circle, and as a byproduct of their closed system, intermarriage became the norm.

My grandparents were actually distant cousins. The boundaries of intermarriage at that time, especially in the area of religion, were as strong as the boundaries of intermarriage between races were forty years ago. One just did not marry outside of one's religion. Even in Tiburda, with its unusually cohesive population, people married between religions less frequently. Eventually, American culture worked its magic, and life in the Tiburda building on Fox Street was not immune; some of those boundaries broke down. There were intermarriages between Muslims, Jews, Russian Orthodox Christians, and the other ethnic minorities.

Opportunities were very different in New York than they were in the old country, where life was much more regulated and limited. Here, opportunities frequently proceeded according to one's capacity. So since my family had a relatively intellectual bent, my father became an attorney, his sister a doctor, and his brother a mechanical engineer. Eventually a socioeconomic separation did take place in this community apartment house, and my family moved uptown, to what is now known as the South Bronx.

They didn't move uptown in a mother-father-kids arrangement. Fifteen years before I was born, ten Tiburdans moved uptown together and rented the whole top floor of an apartment house in the Bronx. They opened up the walls and created one huge apartment, with three separate kitchens and six bathrooms. (I actually slept in a converted kitchen.) A few rooms were broken through to make a living room that could hold all those residing there, plus a copious flow of immigrant visitors from all the different ethnicities represented in my family.

My mother, my father, and my grandparents on both sides all represented different religious traditions, so when my sister, my cousins, and I, came along, there was some competition over just what these kids were going to be. I ended up with a little of this and a little of that, and didn't really get enveloped by any of them.

This scene in which I grew up may seem romantic, even exotic, but it was really very embarrassing for me. I didn't like to bring my friends home, because it was more like a community hall than a house. I would rarely invite a friend over, not being able to explain what was going on there, or answer the questions that kids asked, especially in a time when ethnicity was so important: "So, what are you?"

There was always a stream of immigrants going through the house. My grandparents helped people find places to live, so our apartment became somewhat of a staging point between Ellis Island, where immigrants were placed when they first landed, and some apartment where they eventually were to live. As a child, I remember families, mostly Russian, but some also from Turkey and Armenia, that would stay with us until they got a place of their own. Then they would move out. I don't remember ever having dinner with less than fifteen people, but it wasn't like one big dinner – it was more like cafeteria-style.

When I was nine years old my father died. It was a traumatic experience for me, and really for my whole family. Even though there were a lot of people around, and my grandparents were definitely formidable figures, my father was considered the success of the clan. He was an attorney for the New York Democratic Party. I didn't get to know him very well, but he was looked on as a key person in our family group.

When somebody dies, religions follow different traditional practices. In Islam they have delineated practices, which are different from the customs of Russian Orthodoxy, which in turn are different from those of Judaism. Both my mother and her mother, who might have been considered the matriarch of the family (or at least the major cook, which in many families equals the matriarch) leaned toward the Jewish tradition. Even though they may not have represented the majority numerically, they were both central figures in my life, and also very close to me.

In Judaism, when somebody dies, there is a traditional ritual, and the ritual extends on every day for a year. I'm not sure about the details – it's either the closest male relative, or the oldest male relative, or all the relatives. Whoever it is, they go to the synagogue every day for the next year and say a prayer – the same prayer every day.

By the time I was nine, I had gone to a synagogue a few times. I had also gone to church, and to the mosque a few times. I was not an attender of anything, nor did I feel an affinity or connection to anything but baseball. I was just a regular kid. But it was very important for them, and they impressed upon me that *one does this and you will do this.* I don't remember how this impressing happened, but it probably involved major fear tactics. A child can put forth an amount of resistance, and I probably did, but ultimately I went along with it, maybe because I was so traumatized by the loss of my father.

I began to go to the synagogue every day after school. Basically, there were a lot of old people at these scenes. I was the only kid. I would sit through a service that took about an hour. At the end of the service, they would announce that anyone who had a relative who had died in the last year should stand up. Then almost everyone would stand and say a prayer in a language that I had heard, but knew not one word of – well maybe one or two. Then, wanting of course to be as invisible as possible, I would have to stand up (which I hated – especially in the beginning) with all these old people. The prayer was very long and in a foreign language, so I had to memorize it phonetically, because nobody ever told me what any of the words meant. Eventually I memorized the prayer and could say it pretty fast, which in this particular religious tradition is recognized as a very definite manifestation of piety.

I felt no quality, no depth, no understanding, nor was any put forth to me. Basically I was exercising a tradition, a ritual, a dogma of some kind, only because I was told to do so. I did from time to time have thoughts about my father while in the synagogue, but I probably would have had more of them if I were sitting home. Mostly, I felt awkward and embarrassed, and eventually the year passed, and I was very glad it did.

Even after you say this prayer every day for a year, you're still not done. In subsequent years, you are supposed to go to a synagogue on a particular holiday and do the same thing at a special memorial service.

By coincidence, the very last day of my year-long sentence fell on a holiday called Yom Kippur, the holiest of holy holidays in the Jewish tradition – which, by the way, is accented by the fact that it is a fast day (you know it's big time if Jewish people don't eat). My father had died on this holiday, so when the year was up, it was also on this holiday. On Yom Kippur, not only do the people who have loved ones who died during the year get up and say this prayer, but everybody does it. It's like a mass memorial service which only happens once every year. For the next two years I went to the yearly service, and then I rebelled against that tradition, and most others presented to me, and never went back to a synagogue.

Over the years of my life from then until now, which has been a lot of years, I have studied religions and traditions. If I were to grade those religious traditions for quality, depth, and their ability to maintain any semblance whatsoever of their spiritual origins, I would put Judaism last, and Christianity only slightly ahead. There are some people that I have met – perhaps Jesus freaks or Evangelical Christians, who are still looking for something spiritual in their religion, but not many.

I'll give you an example of what I mean. There are instructions in Judaism that come from the Old Testament, directing farmers, when they harvest their fields, not to harvest the corners, because the corners are to be saved and left in the fields for beggars and strangers – a direction obviously reflecting a beautiful sentiment. If you travel around Israel now, you will see numerous octagonal fields (rectangular fields with the corners cut off). When you ask people how come they are shaped like that, they will tell you they don't know why, other than, it says to do so in the Bible.

All religions, whether they be Buddhist, Christian, or Islamic, contain thousands of rituals that adherents perform and don't know why – or if they do have an explanation *why*, it's not really *why*, it's just what we have grown to believe is *why*, or we have accepted as the explanation *why*. I mention this as an example of the deterioration of that particular religion, and similarly of all the others. That is not to say that their original essence was not extraordinarily beautiful and deeply spiritual – of course it was.

That brings us to last Monday. Last Monday morning I woke up remembering that I needed to figure out my schedule for the upcoming month of October. There is a calendar hanging on my wall, and as I started to look at it, I saw that that very Monday was Yom Kippur. My first thought, of course, was that my father had died on that day so many years before. My next thought was most unexpected, especially in light of my opinions about organized religion. I thought simply, and directly, "I am going to go to the synagogue." Naturally, like everyone else, I have had thoughts about things that I have not done anything about – the resistance is a little too much, there are too many stumbling blocks, and I don't do it. But in this particular case, I went directly to the yellow pages and looked up synagogues. I knew there was a big one somewhere nearby, because some years before I was arranging for a public meeting room and went to a local synagogue to inquire about their facilities. But that was so many years ago, and I didn't even remember where it was. So I called up, and the answering machine said, "Hello, our offices are closed today because of the holiday . . ." and then it went on to give some details about the memorial service – like that it starts sometime between 4-4:30 pm. Knowing what I do about going to large gatherings, I figured that it would be good to get there early, so I arranged to arrive around 3:00 pm.

When I arrived, about 500 people were sitting in long oak pews in the main synagogue, and another room full of folding chairs was annexed onto that room for overflow, because this event attracted the most abundant attendance of the year. Anybody who would ever go to a synagogue would go on this particular day. Usually, I would opt to sit toward the front, but those seats were all either occupied or reserved.

I really didn't know what I wanted, other than to feel something about my father. Sitting in the front is helpful if you want to feel like you're part of a participatory scene, but I felt more in search of a private experience.

I found an unoccupied folding chair near the back where it was sparsely settled, and started to listen. Having traveled extensively, and having been part of so many varied group dynamics over the years, I have learned, and now consider it important, to find value in things however unapparent. So I would try not to walk away from something, even if it were a political meeting, with the attitude that there was nothing of value going on there. We can learn to find something of value almost anywhere, if we can resist finding fault. After all, if there are humans there, there is life there. If there is life there, the Creator is there; maybe it's hard to spot – but it's there.

So there I was, sitting in a synagogue for the first time in over fifty years, watching the activity that was currently happening up front – a sequence of teenagers getting on the *stage* in order to read from their holy book. They were reading in a sing-song tone in a language I doubt they understood, alternating that with passages in English, during which everyone stood up, sat down, stood up, sat down – basically like a church scene.

It was somewhat difficult to concentrate, because not only did the meaning of the English part seem remote, but there was also a tremendous sea of movement in the many rows in between the stage and me – not to mention people talking to each other as they walked around. As I said, sometimes it's hidden, and you really have to put an extra effort into extracting the gems. These were really hidden.

A voice arose in my head saying, "What am I doing here?" That voice began to alternate with another one that said, "Well, you said you were going to be here. Just stay." During this conversation with myself, some people sat down next to me. For some reason, people dress up for this holiday even though it is a memorial day holiday, and the two people who sat next to me were obviously familiar with that part of the tradition – designer prayer shawls included. When they started talking to each other about business, my *you gotta get outta here* voice started to get the upper hand. "What are you doing here? If you want to do this, go home, sit in your room, and think about your father." Still not being prepared to bail on the possibility, I got up and moved to the last row of the overflow, where there was nobody around me.

I looked at my watch and it was 3:30 pm. It was going to be an hour before the memorial service began. How would I spend the time? I decided to read from a copy of the prayer book (*The Siddur*) that was placed on each seat. I figured, as long as I was going to be sitting here, I might as well have a memorial ceremony of my own. I would read the service, and try to feel the feelings and have the experience.

At the beginning of the section of the book called *Yom Kippur Memorial Service,* I found a poem.

> "Lord, I yearn only to be near you. Though at times I seem remote. Lord, I cannot find the way unaided, teach me the faithful service you would have me do. Show me your ways, guide me, lead me, release me from the prison of unknowing while I can still make amends. Do not despise my lowly state before I grow so weak, so heavy with mortality that I bend and fall, and my bones brittle with age become food for moth and worms. Be my help, Oh be my help. Where my forebears went, there I go, yes I know their resting place is mine, I know it. Like them I am a stranger passing through this life. Since the womb of earth is my allotted portion, and since I have chased the wind from the beginning of my days. When will I come to set my house in order? The passions you yourself have made a part of me have kept me wrapped in the passing scene. How enslaved to passion have I been? A prey to fierce and fiery hungers, how I ask could I have served you as I needed to. But now the time has come to ask, why all this ambition, why the quest for high estate? When tomorrow I must die? Why this expense of spirit when tomorrow I mourn the passing time. These days and nights combine to bring me to the end. They scatter my thought to the wind, they return my frame to the dust, what now can I say in my defense, what brave words remain to shield me from my truth? My nature has pursued me, possessed me, driven and flayed me. A doubtful friend from childhood on. What then do I really have besides your presence? Stripped of my pretensions, naked at the last here I stand. And only

your goodness can clothe and shelter me, for nothing now remains but this. Lord, I yearn only to be near you."

At the end of the poem were the Hebrew words written phonetically in English letters, and the English translation. It was the prayer I had said every day for a year when I was ten years old. I reread those beautiful words that were part of the prayer that I had said in a foreign language, never understanding one word, nor was the meaning of one word ever explained to me. I went on to read the rest of the service – it was equally inspiring. After reading it, I stayed for the service and had a wonderfully deep experience. So much arose in me that generally doesn't – thoughts and feelings about people who had died during my life.

I had been so focused on thinking I was going there only in relation to my father who had died years ago on that day, and for whom I had said that prayer, that I hadn't really thought of other people who have had a tremendous influence on my life, and have also passed on. Toward the end of the prayer, thoughts of some of those people arose, along with memories of their faces. It was stirring.

Along with everyone else, I stood and said this ten-minute prayer in Hebrew, still not knowing what any individual word meant, but having a very different experience than I had ever had before. I was really tremendously grateful to have been there – to have followed through and made the phone calls and looked at the calendar – to have sat through the resistance and stayed to the end.

Originally, I was going to include only the poem in this book – it's so powerful in itself. But I started to think of this poem in relation to my life, and it seemed like something

I could tell you about myself in the way of an introduction. There is a very definite bridge of the heart in this story. There is for me; I hope there is for you too.

One of the hardest things to maintain in spiritual work, or spiritual discipline, or self-study, self-knowledge, self-realization, or transcendence, is to take the feelings of the heart into the exercises of the body and the mind. They are so easily lost, because when we talk about what's possible, we talk so much about ideas and methods.

I have tried to study, to learn, to maintain, to preserve, and to teach both the importance and the practicality of having those deep feelings not be relegated to isolated compartments. If we talk about ideas, concepts, philosophies, and disciplines, and lose the essence of those heart feelings, something precious will have been lost – something we never want to lose. Whether we know it or not – more than all other things, we want to feel the love inside of us.

Now that I know the meaning of the words in this Kaddish prayer, I can actually value it, when I repeat it at this moment for:

Jack Gold – my father
Libby Gold – my mother
Raoul Raya Rainti – my mentor
Ann Scarbro Jacobs – my friend
Dick Jacobs – my friend

I invite you to do the same if you wish, for those that are gone, but are still a part of your special memories.

Chapter 11
The Herd Instinct

Let me tell you a story about something that happened in my childhood, and maybe I'll be able to tie it to a theme that we both would consider important. The part of the Bronx where I lived was very near Yankee Stadium, where the New York Yankees played baseball and still do. From the roof of the apartment house I grew up in, you could actually see into the stadium, except for right field. When the Yankees were in the World Series, which was often in the years when I was a kid, people from the neighborhood would pay the maintenance man of our building to go up to our roof and watch. The residents of the building didn't pay; all we had to do was bring up our chairs, radios, and binoculars to hear the play by play and watch the game – except for right field.

When I was in my first year of junior high, I developed the hobby of missing days of school. I would get a note from my mother, go to school, say I was late, and then split. I don't remember the details, but it worked pretty smoothly. One of the things I did when I skipped school, was go to a nearby park with a couple of my friends and make campfires and cook hotdogs. We would take the subway to a place called Van Cortlandt Park, which was further north in the Bronx, and have a little picnic. As this avocation developed, I had to come up with new things to do. One of the things I did during baseball season, was go to Yankee Stadium and sit in the bleachers. The bleachers are concrete stands that don't have actual seats and cost very little. We would sit there for the afternoon and watch the baseball game.

I'm setting the scene for you, because something very profound happened to me at one of these games. It had nothing to do with baseball – sorry to disappoint the fans among you – so no, I didn't catch Mickey Mantle's longest home run ball or anything like that, though I did see him play. Something happened one day that I still remember, so it must have had an effect on me.

As you know now, I grew up in a multi-ethnic background, where my grandparents on both sides were combinations of Russian Orthodox Christian, Jewish, and Muslim. I went, depending on who had dibs on influencing me that particular weekend, to the church, the synagogue, or the mosque. It wasn't really that bad, but even so, when I got to the age of around 11 or 12, there were more attractive things for me to do, so I became disinterested and didn't go to those places of worship anymore.

Since my family had been involved with so many of the people in the community (everyone called my grandparents *Mom* and *Pop,* so they must have been central figures in the community), religious leaders would come to our house. We had a very large apartment, and there was always a big gang there for dinner, sometimes a very big gang.

In the beginning, I was a little in awe of these rabbis, priests, and imams, especially some of them who spoke different languages. After a while I lost interest, maybe because they were noisy, and there was a lot of arguing. I didn't like bringing my friends home either, because it was embarrassing for me. I didn't like the scene, and eventually I didn't think much of those religious leaders. Maybe it was their sanctity, or the consistency of their personality, but I had developed a negative opinion about their manner.

Let's skip back to the day that I went to the baseball game. I was sitting in the bleachers with a couple of my friends, and I spotted a Russian Orthodox priest that had been to my house, and I had been to his church. He looked fully the all-in-black bearded Russian Orthodox priest. He was shouting and cursing, rooting for the Yankees. I was watching him really carry on, and lost complete interest in the baseball game. I was fascinated watching the enthusiasm and the inconsistency of this person that I thought was basically one thing, a Russian Orthodox priest – definitely not one of the more liberal of callings.

I wasn't reclaimed by the church, and I didn't reexamine my values, but those impressions of him did stick with me, so when I saw him at other times after that, I remember being a little more curious about this person. Maybe I became curious because of a theory that I've heard about – the *herd instinct* – as in a herd of buffalos, a herd of cattle, something like that.

What I've seen, is that the influences on us from the time we are children are so impactful, that we adopt concepts that help us form our idea of the life we want to lead. These concepts are always picked up externally – from the internet,

TV, people, movies, books, from whatever impressions we take in. We gather bits of information about what it is like to be a such and such, and each one of us has our individual such and such, an international spy, a good homemaker, a movie star, a computer engineer, a spiritual seeker, or whatever.

We are constantly gathering the external impressions of what it would look like to be the particular type of person that we aspire to be. *They eat this kind of food, ah ha! They wear these kinds of clothes, ah ha! They read these kinds of books, talk in this way, think about these things.* After we get to a certain age, we have a fairly comprehensive picture of what has to be done to be like this person. Nothing actually has transpired as yet, but we have gathered a concept of what we are supposed to look like, of what we are supposed to sound like, how we are to act, how we can impress other people, down to really miniscule details. Whatever group or herd we wish to become part of begins to dictate our actions.

As we start to take on these ways of being, we imagine that we're being a totally unique individual, because we don't see that we've adopted concepts through our observation of others. We see this about others when we hear about stereotypes like *The Man in the Grey Flannel Suit.* We see the expense accounts, the bars, the plane travel, the business conventions, and the way of competing in the office, and judge those people as clones of each other. We see those things about other people, but we don't see that about ourselves; in fact, we think that we are exempt from being part of a herd.

Each of us has the concept that whatever we've taken on has been taken on uniquely and individually. We don't realize that we've become a captive audience to the herd that we want to be part of. In actuality, every aspect of our behavior, of our life, of our possessions, of our mannerisms, have been adopted because of this herd instinct.

When I was confronted with the inconsistency of this priest rooting for a baseball team, and shouting with enthusiasm, acting completely incompatible with the rest of his herd, it meant to me that there was something original and unique there – something that came from within him. After that, it was obvious that the herd instinct I had begun to see in myself and others needed to be examined.

Even though we have unconsciously become part of a herd, we are all, equally unconsciously terrified, that by becoming part of a herd we'll lose something. What we don't understand, is that what we fear happening has already happened. We have already relinquished our individuality. We have relinquished our uniqueness. We're not the unique experiment on the part of nature that we imagine ourselves to be. We are part of a herd. We are indistinguishable parts of a herd, but we see it otherwise.

We're always asking, "How does my age fit in? How does my appearance fit in? How does my gender fit in? How does my profession fit in? How does my socio-economic position fit it? How does my marital status fit in? How does my parental status fit in? How does my hair color fit in? How does my nose length fit in? How does my weight fit in?" Fit into what? Your herd, of course.

You laugh, but these questions are always on your mind, and you check them off, not even knowing that you're checking them off. You ask these questions rather than feeling your own life, feeling the individuality of your own life, and letting *that* express how you fit in. There is a misconception that a rugged individualist is exempt from such limitations, but even a rugged individualist is part of a rugged individualist herd. A rugged individualist herd has extremely rigid requirements – you can't be around any other rugged individualists. Your herd is not a visible one, but it has group gatherings from time to time – except nobody goes. That's how you know it's a rugged individualist herd – everybody bad-mouths the gatherings and nobody goes.

I have lived on the West Coast for more years now than I had lived on the East Coast, but even though I was clearly removed physically, I spent the first few years after I moved, steadfastly maintaining my claim of membership in the New Yorker herd – not out of loyalty as one might like to think – but out of insecurity.

When we change a few variables in our life, we try to convince ourselves that everything is new and fresh. But it's not new and fresh, it's only a revised herd. For a while it may appear to be new and fresh, but there is so much repetition, so much mimicry, so much imitation, and so much herding that any potential originality gets lost.

There's something that's gone off course here. We've lost the thread of appreciating originality. We've lost the thread of what unique expression is. Everyone has a flair. Everyone's flair isn't flamboyant, but everyone has a flair. Everyone is a unique experiment on the part of nature – not *almost* everyone, *everyone* is a unique experiment on the part of nature – every single one.

Chapter 12

The Flute

I was in Peru in the 1980s with some friends. We spent a few months hiking and climbing around at some higher elevations in the Andes mountains. We started off in the north, around Huaraz in the Cajon de Huaylache Mountains, and did some climbing and camping on the slopes of 20,000 foot Mt. Jirishanca. After that we went south to Cusco. People know Cusco because that's where you go to get to Machu Pichu, the famous Inca ruins. We didn't go there, but instead went south and climbed to the top of Nevado Ausangate. I had been to Peru before, but never to these particular mountains.

I'm bragging about my mountain climbing accomplishments because they explain why, when we eventually returned to Cusco, we were all very tired, had lost a lot of weight, and needed some good R & R in this lovely town in the Andes mountains. One day, I was walking around and looking in the shops, thinking I might buy a flute. I had only been playing the flute for a short while. It was the most recent of my musical instrument explorations – explorations that began with the violin when I was three years old, and went on to include saxophone, piano, drums, harmonica, guitar, and now flute. I actually learned to play the flute from Linda, a friend who was on this trip. She played the silver flute. I had made a flute some years before, but had never really played it. I guess it wasn't time yet.

One day I borrowed Linda's silver flute and made some sounds that I really liked. I was walking around the streets of Cusco and saw a little shop belonging to a guy who made flutes. Flutes are very basic to Andean music. If you've heard some of that outrageously wonderful music, you know that the basic instruments are pan pipes, drums, flutes and little mandolin-like instruments. Most of the flutes made and played in the Andes are called *quenas*. They have a slot you blow across the top of, instead of sideways, like a silver flute. A traditional flute was difficult enough for me, but I found making any sound (other than air) out of a *quena* impossible. This guy had probably fifty *quenas* in his window that he had made, plus one wooden flute that blew sideways like a silver flute.

I'm going to digress a bit, for those of you who have traveled in third world countries and know something about *bargaining*. The creed of the hip, world traveler is, *you are always supposed to bargain*. If they say, "Two dollars," you say, "One dollar," and you feel great satisfaction from depriving this person of a day's worth of food, because you bargained successfully. In more affluent countries, bargaining is *verboten,* at least we have been told that it isn't done, so we have gotten into the habit of either paying what it says on the price tag, or walking out.

We had already been in Peru for three months – that adds up to a lot of bargaining – like every time you go into town . . . vegetables, you bargain, eggs, you bargain. You're always bargaining. At the end of each of my trips to Peru, I have come back with alpaca ponchos and rugs. When you buy tourist-oriented stuff, bargaining is probably indicated, but when you're buying fruit and vegetables, stuff like that, it's probably not, but those of us who have gotten the bargaining bug in third world countries – we do it anyway.

So, I went into this store and pointed out the flute that I was interested in. The man handed it to me to play, and I proceeded to make some lovely sounds on my first try. Next step, ask the price. He asked for the equivalent of eight dollars in Peruvian Soles. Of course, in the true spirit of an American asshole, I responded with whatever the equivalent was in Soles of five dollars. He smiled, shook his head, and said, "No." Then I parried with the equivalent of six dollars in Soles. Once again he smiled, shook his head, and said, "No."

Of course at that point I saw him as breaking the *must bargain* convention. Instead, he suggested I play the flute some more. Once again I tried it, and made some even prettier sounds than I had before. Once again I repeated my offer, and once again he refused. He clearly was not going to bargain. So somewhat self-righteously, I walked out of the shop – proving to myself, later, that I am capable of doing something really foolish.

I walked out and went back to the place where we were staying. That night we went out to eat and listen to some music. Walking around afterward, I started thinking how stupid it was to walk away from that flute. Where would I ever find a handmade instrument like that? It wasn't one of those cheap bamboo flutes – it was quality. So I decided to go back the next day – maybe offer him the equivalent of seven dollars. Even if I had to pay full price, I'd get the flute. When we got back to our room, we drank some *pisco,* and I told everybody the story, and we all had a good laugh out of it.

The next day I had things to do, so I didn't get to the shop till the afternoon. I went in and reminded him that I was the guy who was looking at that flute there yesterday, and was still interested in it. He told me that someone had come in earlier and bought it. I felt even more dimwitted than I had before. I asked him if he had any others like that one, and he told me that he rarely made them, because people play *quenas*. I asked him if he could make one for me, and he told me that he would have to find a special kind of wood, but if I came back early next year (it was then November), he might be able to have one for me. I walked out with an awesome feeling of regret, and an equally awesome lesson. I was really disappointed.

I went back and told my friends what had happened. We had a good discussion about lessons and learning, and how sometimes pain is a good teacher. Soon afterward, we flew back to California. By then the pain of my blunder had somewhat left me, and I was left with the lesson.

We got back about a week or so before Thanksgiving, and my birthday. A few of my friends threw a birthday party for me; there were about a dozen people there – the people who had gone to Peru and a few others. The flute was long gone, and the pain was less gone, but I wasn't thinking about that much anymore.

We had the candles in the cake, and the *Happy Birthday to You* song, after which people were handing me boxes and things. After reading one of the cards – it was from Linda – I started unwrapping the present that went with it. She asked me to guess what it was before I opened it. I didn't have a clue what it was. I tore off the paper and opened the long narrow box. It was the flute. I don't think I could describe how happy seeing that flute made me. Not only did I learn an important lesson, but I didn't have to suffer for very long after it, thanks to a remarkable gesture from a remarkable friend.

I don't want to tarnish this love story with a lengthy moral, so here's a short one: We all have habits and ways we have done things in the past. Many of them are useful practices that have developed out of necessity and can be applied to our benefit. But if our actions are repeated unconsciously, that is, without asking ourselves whether they are appropriate for the moment, we will sometimes cause ourselves unnecessary suffering.

Chapter 13
Two Floyds

The New York City of my childhood was made up of multicultural neighborhoods where Irish, Jewish, Italian, and Puerto Rican families lived, but in my immediate neighborhood very few black people (then referred to as Negroes) lived.

Most black people lived in Harlem, which was probably 30 or 40 blocks away from where I lived, so I didn't go to school with black kids, but I did go to school with kids of all the other nationalities that I mentioned.

The multicultural nature of my family probably reduced the amount of prejudice that I was exposed to, but it was still there. I did have some very consequential exposure to black people as a child – a couple of them anyway. One was Maude, the maid who worked in my house, and who I had known from my earliest memories. It took me a while to understand the perspective that she was racially different from me, because I was actually darker than she was. She was black and I was white, and I got to know that story. She was part of my household, and I liked her. She took care of me, and did different things that I appreciated. I guess you could say that we became friends, at least from a child's point of view.

Another black person I got to know as a little kid was Floyd. He worked at my family's restaurant as a cook and pot washer. In addition to a restaurant, my family also owned a summer house on a lake a few hours outside of the city. Before the summer season began, my father and I would open up the lake house, and do everything that had to be done to get it livable. Floyd would always come with us. One of my sweetest memories from childhood is spending time with my father and also with Floyd. The three of us would play ball and go out fishing together. Floyd was actually the one who taught me how to play poker, which eventually had a fairly consequential influence on my life. When I went to my family's restaurant during the school year, I would go back into the kitchen, and Floyd would let me help him cook and wash pots. Even now, from time to time, when I'm washing a pot I think about Floyd, and I'm going to tell you a little bit about why.

Some years later I lived in Greenwich Village in New York. I did different things to make money, some of them around gambling, and some around other semi-illegal activities. Between where I lived and some of the businesses I dealt with was a street corner I passed a couple of times a week where homeless people hung out. At that time, maybe a less compassionate time, homeless people were known as winos. I don't know if that meant they were alcoholics or not alcoholics, but we didn't call them homeless people. We called them winos, and it was not a complimentary term. One of the guys who was there almost every time I passed by, became the beneficiary of my minimal charitable instinct.

This particular guy would panhandle for spare change with his hat balanced in front of him on top of a beer mug. I remember liking the anomaly. I would give him a dollar, and sometimes talk to him a little. After a while I developed an affinity for this person – especially when I found out his name was Floyd. He certainly wasn't the same Floyd, nor did I imagine that he was, as he was quite a bit older than the Floyd of my childhood would have been.

Putting money in his hat evoked a sweet memory for me, and for a while I got to feel like a caring person – the rest of the time I certainly was not. It couldn't have been that invigorating, because my charity went only to the point that I would contribute a dollar to him a couple of times a week, and that's about it.

A few days before Christmas, I was walking by Floyd's corner and got an idea (certainly not because of my sweet and charitable soul, but more because it gave me pleasure). Some people get pleasure by doing things for other people, and some people get pleasure from taking things from other people, but it's all personal pleasure. Of course, one is helpful, and the other hurtful, so in that way they are clearly not the same.

It was my personal pleasure to take a liking to Floyd, and help him out to the small extent that I did. So, I was walking by Floyd's corner and got the idea that I would give him a big chunk of money, and see what he did with it. He was lying on a bench snoozing with his big ex-army jacket on, so I took five $100 bills, rolled them into a ball, put the money in his jacket pocket, and walked away without him waking up.

A few days later I went to Florida for that winter. It was probably a couple of months later that I returned to New York, and I heard the sad story that Floyd had died. Floyd was a fixture around Greenwich village, so the people that owned businesses and walked around there all knew him, or at least knew that the wino on the corner with the hat on the beer mug was gone. The story was confusing, because Floyd was found in a poverty-stricken situation, but $500 was found in his pocket – the money that I had given him two months before. The money was crumpled up with a bunch of newspaper in his jacket.

Homeless people sometimes use newspaper to insulate themselves on cold nights, so Floyd had filled his jacket with newspaper to have some insulation from the cold. He must have stuffed newspaper over the hundred-dollar bills, and thought they were just more paper, so he didn't even know they were there. He had access to going to a warm hotel, eating some decent food, changing his life to some degree, at least temporarily, but he wasn't aware that he had this treasure in his pocket, so he couldn't take advantage of it. He died, not knowing that at least he could have had some relief. Maybe he even died as a result of exposure to cold. He died in terrible circumstances on that bench, when he didn't have to. That extra suffering at the end of his life was really unnecessary, but any other possibility was unknown to him.

I thought of Floyd this morning while I was washing a dish – the first Floyd of my childhood, not the second Floyd. I had recently visited that lake in New York for the first time since I had left as a child. I thought about Floyd and me playing ball and playing poker and stuff like that. Thinking about the first Floyd brought only positive feelings. Then, for some reason, I thought about the second Floyd. I couldn't avoid thinking of the sadness, and the irony of his circumstances – having a treasure in his pocket totally accessible to him, and not using it.

I'm telling you this story because there is an extraordinary parallel between the second Floyd's life and plight, and the plight of human beings on this earth right now. Hundreds of billions of creatures have come and gone – from tiny ones, to huge ones, to humans, to domesticated animals, to fish – all kinds of creatures have come and gone.

All animal life can be grouped into two categories. The first covers all the creatures including humans, bugs, fish, dogs, sheep, dinosaurs, and all those bestowed with the will to take care of themselves – to provide nourishment and comfort and security for themselves. All these creatures are involved with the quest for what I call grounding, and have some capacity to achieve it. For some creatures it is a very tenuous grounding, as they are in frequent danger, but they are always trying to create a nest for themselves, a safe nest, a nurturing nest, a comfortable nest.

In the second category, there are only human beings. No other creature is bestowed with the capacity to be aware of where their life comes from – to be conscious of where life comes from – to be conscious of what's happening around them in actuality. Human beings can do something in addition to self-protection, in addition to grounding – only human beings have this capacity. The tragedy is that this capacity is tucked in the pocket of human life, with so much insulation stuffed in with it, and over it.

Human beings seek pride in all kinds of accomplishments: being beautiful, being competent, being talented, being dexterous, even being proud of their ability to clean a toilet. *I am the best at that! I am the best at that sport! I am the best at this intellectual pursuit. I am a good dancer.* Humans are always seeking pride in different things, not realizing that being proud to be an American, being proud to be a Brit, being proud to be an Indian, or a Pakistani, or a South African, or a Batswani is only another variety of *look at me*.

We have a built-in natural pride that is not separating like all those other prides are, because *I am that* and *you are not that*. The pride that's natural to us is the pride of being a human being – the good fortune of being a human being. *I am proud to be a human being*. Where does one ever hear that idea? It is a pride that creates no separation between people in any way whatsoever, because we are all human beings, and we will never better that gift.

But that natural pride is hidden in our pocket, and all the newspaper of life is stuffed on top of it, and we are unaware of it. We are so unaware of it, that our pursuits for fulfillment are reduced to the pursuits of fame, and wealth, and comfort. We spend all of our time pursuing something to be proud of, something that will allow us to be loved, something that will allow us to love, something that will make it so that we are not lonely – so that we're not bored.

We don't realize that we have a secret in our pocket. The pursuit and realization of our natural connection to the force that gives us life is our natural birthright. It is available to us, but it has become hidden. There is something that can hold the weight of our lives. It is not our relationships, not our assets, not our possessions, not our activities, not our talents – none of these can hold the weight of our lives. None of these can do it. When we lean the weight of our lives on those things, those relationships falter, those talents falter, those assets falter. That same wealth and those possessions that we have sacrificed for become burdens to us. They are not meant to hold the weight of our lives. They are meant to add joy and variety to our lives, but not to hold the weight.

Something hidden in our pocket is meant to hold that weight. Our natural gift as human beings grants us access to knowing, in the moment, that life is coming into us and that we are being cared for. That is what can hold the weight of our lives. Not in a personal way, but in a much more encompassing way – like our sun is taking care of us. It's not only giving us vitamin D, it's warming our earth, not because it loves us in the way we ordinarily think of love, but because it and we are part of the same creation.

Chapter 14
The Gorilla

Embarrassment is what we experience when the image we have worked to project to others is unexpectedly disrupted. I have called those moments *little deaths,* but they are really not so little. We are so attentive to not letting those moments happen, that we have become addicted to the ways we avoid them. There is an expression used to describe the burden of people's addictions – "Having a monkey on your back." It's a pictorially graphic saying, which would be even more graphic if it were a gorilla on your back. That is more accurately the case, in the example of the compulsion to avoid the embarrassment of threatened self-image.

The difference between a monkey and a gorilla is about 500 pounds. Kids carry book-bags the weight of a monkey to school on their backs day after day, and soon can even get used to the weight to a point where they are unaware that they are carrying anything extra. Try that with a gorilla.

Imagine how consistently we must have labored, to become oblivious to the weight of a gorilla that makes demands of us in every moment – in all our responses, and every place we go. It insists that we be attentive to how we look, to what we say, to what we let on about what we're doing, all in dedication to the protection of our image, our reputation. Its insistence even carries to the moment when we accidentally slip and take a minor fall. It insists that we immediately look around to determine if our awkwardness has been seen by others, because we certainly don't want to appear clumsy.

I have a kidney stone. It's on the left side. I was in Europe about seven years ago when I found out that I had this kidney stone. All of a sudden I had an intense pain in my lower left back, that radiated around the front as well. It didn't feel quite like indigestion or anything else I had ever felt, and it wouldn't go away. It wasn't in the appendix area, so it wasn't that, and it wasn't muscular, but I didn't know what it was.

The people I was traveling with had some very anxious moments, wondering if they should take me to the hospital, or what. We were all at a loss for what to do, until I got some relief from ibuprofen. Later that day I spent some time Googling my pain, and it became clear what was causing it – at least a lot clearer than it was earlier.

I still have the same kidney stone, and even though it's bigger now, and sometimes hurts as much as it did then – it's different – because I'm used to it now. Now, I'm not thinking about what to do about it. Do I go to the hospital?

What should I take? Because I'm used to it. I've learned to live with it. It doesn't hurt all the time, but every few weeks it hurts for an hour or so. It has become part of my reality, like this gorilla on your back may have become part of yours.

To really understand this particular burden that we're carrying, is also to recognize why the quest for freedom is such an uphill battle for us. We pursue self-improvement, thinking that something can really come of it. We fail to understand that we're going to a seminar, or we're using a particular method, and all the time, there's a gorilla on our back. We wonder why nothing really works. Those attempts, though sincere, are doomed to failure, because the gorilla is always there, and we're unaware of its presence.

We must recognize that unless we can contend with this burden of pride, with this self-image, with this fear of being seen in any way, even 1% away from the way we want to be seen, all other attempts will be fruitless. We are perpetually occupied with the question, "I know how I want to appear. What do I have to do to appear that way?" So we avoid situations that are unknown or unpredictable, because we don't know how to work it so that we can appear the way we want to.

If we can't avoid those situations, we research them before hand to find out: "Who's going to be there? What's it going to be like? What will I be called on to do?" The gorilla insists that we have to protect and defend our self-image, and we obey it religiously. We're uneasy not being in control of our own image. Acting to regain that control dictates our behavior in so many of the moments of our life. A person can get used to almost anything; obviously the pain of a kidney stone, even the weight of a monkey on our back – but a gorilla? – hard to believe.

You know by now that I grew up in New York City. Eventually my family moved to the suburbs of Westchester County, but I was still enamored of the city. I was too young to travel into the city and hang out there by myself, so when I wasn't in school, I hung out at the local YMCA with my friends, and played pool and ping pong.

As soon as I could, probably around 18 years old, I moved to mid-town Manhattan, and the city became the place where I lived. The suburbs were a very different environment from the city. Among other things, Manhattan was where all the pool pros and the hustlers were. I was pretty good at pool, especially for a kid in the suburbs, but compared to those pros and hustlers, I wasn't very good at all. Fortunately for me, I was smart enough to know it.

Broadway was the most exciting place possible. I loved hanging out in one particular pool room where show business types, people in the boxing world, and gamblers congregated. You might picture a pool room being a dark and seedy place, but it wasn't like that. It was actually a relatively sophisticated place. Hanging out there, I eventually got to know some hustlers, some sports people, and even some show business people. One of the people that I met was an actor early in his career named Peter Falk, who you probably know from his later role as Colombo on TV.

We became acquaintances – not more than that – he was quite a bit older than I. I think he liked my confident attitude, and we also had some family similarities in our background. He wasn't at all like the characters he played. He was well-educated, very intelligent, and had a master's degree. He sometimes hung around the pool room because it was near the Broadway theater district.

On one occasion, we were playing pool and talking, until eventually he had to leave. He told me that he had some friends who were putting together a show for an off-Broadway theater in Greenwich Village. They were holding auditions in a theater around the corner on Broadway. He asked if I wanted to take a walk over there with him and watch the auditions. I had no real interest in the theater, and probably hadn't been to a Broadway show since my mother took me to Carousel when I was nine, but I enjoyed walking the streets of mid-town Manhattan, so we walked together to this theater.

When we walked into the theater it was dark and empty, except for a few people in the front few rows. I sat down next to Peter somewhere in the middle of the theater. The auditions were very similar to how they are depicted on TV or in the movies. There were a few people sitting in the first rows, and eventually people came up on the stage and read parts from a script, like they were performing.

I watched this for about thirty minutes, and in that time people auditioned for several different parts. Without looking over at me, Peter whispered, "You ought to go for that role." I thought he was joking, as getting up there was not in any way in my thoughts, so I ignored him and just laughed. Then, with a voice somewhat louder he said, "You ought to try for this role, you're perfect for it, you're who they're looking for." His suggestion was truly a non sequitur, because being an actor was not in any of my fantasies. My personal concept of celebrity was very different than being in show business.

I wasn't scared or nervous, I wasn't prepared, I wasn't anything. I had never acted in anything ever, nor had I ever thought of doing that. After the second poke, I said okay. He got up, went down front, and talked to the director who was running the audition. The name of the play was going to be *Eh.* No kidding, that was the name. I walked up on the stage having nothing to lose. I didn't know anybody in the place except Peter, and I wasn't feeling like I had to substantiate my acting capacity for him, because he didn't think of me in that way.

I went for it 100%. I really went for it. It was a dramatic role, and as I was reading holding the script in one hand, my other hand was waving around wildly. I was carrying on and having fun doing it. For those five minutes I was playing that part to the max. The director said thank you, and as I started to walk off the stage and go back to my seat next to Peter, he asked me to wait there a minute.

He turned around and called for Peter to come over to him. I was standing there alone on the stage as he was talking to Peter. I don't remember what I was thinking about, but it probably was *that was fun* and *what am I going to do when I leave the theater – go out to eat?* or something like that. After a minute or so, Peter walked up on stage and told me, "He wants you to do it. He wants to give you the part."

It was one of those moments in life when the future flashed before me. I'll tell you what I did, but it's not the most important part of the story, or why I'm telling you about this event. I saw this progression of events happening. I saw this future that I had really no attraction to, or interest in, opening up in front of me, and capturing me, and taking me somewhere that I had no interest in going. It was like a terrorist had kidnapped me in that moment, and told me that the rest of my life was going to be colored by this moment – a moment when I happened to be sitting in a theater next to somebody called Peter Falk.

Moments after Peter said the last word, “part,” I turned, ran down the steps, up the aisle, and out of the theater. I did not walk, I ran. That is the truth – I ran out of the theater. The play turned out to be an award-winning off-Broadway production, starring Dustin Hoffman. The role that I was auditioning for was not his role, because he was quite a bit older than I. I don’t know who played the role I was reading for. I never looked into it, and I never went to see the play.

The lesson, that a person should follow his or her own light, and not be seduced by one that is supposed to be more glamorous or attractive, is an important one, but it is not why I have included this bit of biography here. The reason that I’m recounting this story here, is because the power of having nothing to lose, is a power that is freed when the gorilla is silenced.

In this story, the gorilla was silenced only because of the unique circumstances, and the peculiarities of my personal style as a young man. It was only later that I learned how to silence the gorilla regardless of circumstance. Only that silencing can be considered freedom. What can happen if you’re not carrying that gorilla on your back is unlimited. Without the burden of pride, the force of endangered reputation, the force of wondering what people think – a person could be or do what really called out to them – both in the moment, and for a life’s work. Hey, maybe *you* could be in the movies.

You're not aware of the gorilla being on your back, because it has been there for as long as you can remember. It was there in elementary school, it was there in junior high, it certainly was there in high school, it was there after that, and it's there now. It has become a familiar appurtenance to your body. You've learned how to carry it, appease, and serve it. No matter who you are, even if you would like to claim exemption because of something you've done, you have not relieved yourself of this burden. If I were in front of you now, you would feel somewhat embarrassed, because I'm saying that you're carrying this burden, and you would like to appear that you're not. You would like to appear, that in some way you have gotten free of this burden – at least mostly.

There are other burdens that we carry as well, but none so invasive, none so all-encompassing in its effect on our behavior, as the gorilla of self-image, and pride, and fear of embarrassment. Even when you're alone in your room, you're preparing for your next interaction, in order to prevent your image from being tarnished. You're not aware that you're preparing, but you are rehearsing for it, you're putting together how you will perform, what you will say, what you will do, what you will look like, how you will come across. It doesn't matter if you're going to see someone that you don't know, or someone you call a friend. It doesn't matter if you're in front of the clerk at Safeway. It doesn't matter if it's the person smogging your car. It doesn't matter if it's a small, medium, or large interaction. Your image, or at least some component of it, is at stake in that interaction, and you are burdened by the gorilla of protecting that image.

If you don't think it's as big a problem as I'm putting forth, I have to tell you about a radio interview I was listening to. It was of a lady who had written a biographical book about some experiences she had as a child. She was talking about learning to swim, which is an interesting subject for me, because I was a lifeguard at a summer camp and taught kids how to swim. She was telling the story about how her father taught her how to swim, which was from the old school, by tossing the kid in the water, and hoping the kid would learn how to swim, which I guess sometimes works.

It happened at a pool party at her house with all her friends there. She was six years old, and all her friends were either standing around the pool, or the ones who knew how to swim were in the pool. Her father, without any preamble, without any warning, pitched her in the deep end of the pool.

Now, she is about thirty-five or so, but still has a vivid memory of that moment. She was precisely describing how she was struggling and struggling to stay afloat, and she looked up and saw her father looking at her. Then she looked at her friends, and they were watching her flail around in the water. She was kind of staying above the water, until at some point she couldn't struggle anymore, and she started to go under. What she remembered clearly, was looking up from under the water and seeing her friends standing at the edge of the pool, but they were a little distorted because she was under water. She was going down, not being able to save herself, and her overwhelming feeling was that of being embarrassed. She described this really clearly – it didn't sound like she was exaggerating.

She was drowning, and her overwhelming feeling was embarrassment about looking stupid in front of her friends.

Of course her father jumped in and pulled her out. I used to call embarrassment a *little death,* but this story takes that concept to a whole different level.

Now you know one of the reasons that you're tired at the end of the day, at the end of the week, at the end of the month. It's from this nonstop addiction, this carrying a gorilla on your back, and what makes it worse is that you're unaware of its presence. You imagine that you're tired from other things. You imagine that you're tired from whatever physical work you do, or from business that you have, or from some time-crunch in your schedule. You're not understanding that what you're tired from, is the weight of this gorilla that you're carrying around – one that you are appeasing nonstop.

Chapter 15
Viva Dulio

When I was about 20, I had a religious experience. I'm using the term religious experience, and you're probably jumping to a conclusion. My idol at that time was from neither of the three religions that I was exposed to, nor was my idol anyone political. He was a fictional character from a movie – a man called Henry Gondorff. Paul Newman played him in *The Sting*. He was the ultimate con man – the epitome of a grifter, and he was my idol. I was fascinated with something about the mystique of his lifestyle, and what he did. I spent my late teens and early twenties pursuing that lifestyle with some amount of success; I was a bright kid and became the Henry Gondorff of my peers.

This pursuit took me through a few different activities, and led me to becoming temporarily interested in boxing. I got attracted to boxing through the gambling surrounding that sport. I was an aspiring gambler and bookie and pursued those vocations when I lived in New York. One of the things that I did in that life, was both bet on and book bets on boxing. At that time (not so much now, unless it's a world championship fight) there was a considerable amount of gambling on boxing. At one point, I decided that the place to really get the information was to go into the gym where the boxers trained.

I started to hang out at the gym on the west side of Manhattan where a lot of the boxers who fought in New York at St. Nicolas arena or Madison Square Garden trained. Becoming a true Henry Gondorff requires thoroughness and impeccability, so going to the gym to watch boxers train became part of my gambling research.

I was hanging around there, and after a while (you can just hang around for a certain amount of time before it becomes boring), I started to work out there myself – not the boxing part, but with the weights and punching bags. I liked talking to the trainers and the boxers, and seeing what information I could get. In doing that, I befriended a Puerto Rican guy who was probably about 10 years older than I – his name was Dulio. He looked a little bit beat up. He could have been an ex-boxer, but I didn't know that for sure. I really didn't know anything about him, until one day he said, "Hey, why don't you work out on the heavy bag and the speed bag?" I got to doing that, plus a little jumping rope, and I got fairly decent at all those exercises. That's how I got to know Dulio. He would give me pointers in how to hit the speed bag, and the heavy bag, and jump rope, and all those training tools.

We got to become friends, but mostly friends in the gym. In the middle of the gym there was a boxing ring like you've seen in the movies. Fighters would get in there to spar. They would wear considerable head gear, so they couldn't really get hurt, but they certainly could get hit. I don't know if you know what the headgear looks like, but it covers up some of your face and the side of your eyes. After we knew each other for a couple of months, Dulio asked me if I would like to spar. I asked him with whom? He said, "I'll spar with you. Don't worry, I'm not going to hurt you, and you're probably not going to hurt me."

So I said okay. He was a bigger guy than I. I weighed at that time about 135 lbs, which is a *lightweight*, and he was more like a *middleweight*, which is 160 lbs, and a few inches taller than I. I figured it was okay, because we were just going to fool around in there. We got in the ring, and I put on the head gear and the oversized training gloves. We were jabbing and fooling around, and he was teaching me how to move around in the ring. He tagged me a couple of times, but it didn't really hurt – well maybe a little.

People were stopping what they were doing in order to stand around the ring and watch, and I was sure they weren't watching me. Guys started shouting, "Viva Dulio!" That's what they were saying, "Viva Dulio." I had no idea what was going on, so I stopped and asked him what this *Viva Dulio* business was all about.

It turned out that Dulio was Obdulio Nunez, an accomplished professional boxer who even fought in main events, until he retired five years before because of an eye injury. We became friends, and would go out to eat together, and do things like that. It was interesting for me, because I grew up in the South Bronx, and the relationship between the Puerto Ricans and everybody else was strained. It didn't matter if you were Irish, or Jewish, or Italian, or whatever. The Puerto Ricans were the enemy, and you didn't go into their very defined neighborhood. I had definitely grown up with what you might call a racial bias toward Puerto Ricans, and here I was, making friends with a Puerto Rican boxer. I liked him. He was a thoughtful guy. He had a lot of good boxing stories. I even went to his house and met his wife and kids.

Dulio and I were both upset when the gym began looking to change its image from a boxing gym to a health club. That's where the money was. Gyms at that time were not called health clubs, and they didn't cater to white-collar clientele. That trend began with Nautilus some years later. The owners of this gym must have been in the avant-garde of that movement, because they did some refurbishing in hopes of attracting a higher class of customers than boxers.

They also eventually raised their rates, commensurate to what they wanted to accomplish. I, like everyone else, was self-righteously indignant, and refused to pay more than I was paying, but I did want to continue to use the facilities to train, so I came up with a Henry Gondorff plan. I was looking in the newspaper to see if there were any other gyms with boxing rings, and I saw an ad in the newspaper for a gym for women only – an unusual occurrence for the time. I was sure there was no ring there, but it did light the spark that gave birth to my eventual scheme.

My present gym was proposing a fee hike from $150 a year to $300 a year. The ladies-only gym that I was reading about was obviously trying to get off the ground, because it was advertising membership for $50 a year per person, if three people applied together. So Dulio, and another boxer friend of ours, and I worked up a plan. A few days later, the three of us went to this ladies' gym and said we wanted to join. They, of course, told us of their women-only policy. We asked to speak to the manager.

The context of the time in which this was taking place is important to note. This was a time when affirmative action still hadn't been heard of, but was brewing. There were some organized fledgling black liberation and Puerto Rican liberation movements, and women's issues were also becoming part of the public debate. Discriminatory practices were beginning to become evident. My response to the manager was that their policy was outrageous and discriminatory. I carried on for a few minutes, and then we walked out incensed. Of course this act was part of the plan.

My mother and father were both attorneys. When my father was alive, they both wrote a column for a New York newspaper giving legal advice to veterans. When my mother remarried, she quit her legal career, but she didn't dispose of her legal stationery which I utilized from time to time. She didn't know it, but she became my lawyer – she didn't have anything to do with it, only her stationary did. She (I) wrote a letter as my attorney, saying that we are considering filing a discrimination suit for etc. etc. etc., and I mailed it to the gym manager that I had talked to.

Our plan was to mail three letters in three successive weeks, each one more threateningly escalated. We got no response to the first two. The third letter we sent said we had filed action with the Superior Court, and they had until such a date to respond or this action would go into effect. I didn't know if that was the way it actually worked, but it sounded good.

A few days later, Dulio got a phone call from the attorney for the gym, reaffirming that they couldn't change their women only policy, but offering to pay for the three of our memberships at any gym of our choice in New York. I don't know what feeling Henry Gondorff would have had, but my momentary feeling was elation. The three of us got together for a high-fiving celebration session.

We were sitting around congratulating ourselves till that ran its course. We decided to go the next day and check out the most expensive gym in the city, and join. That night I was sitting in my apartment asking myself if I wanted to join a different gym. I really liked the grubby boxing gym I belonged to. Did I want to hang out with advertising executives from the east side? Why did I do this? What did I get?

I really started to examine my successful conquest. What was it that I had earned? I had achieved my Henry Gondorff plan – the phone call, the letter writing – a complete success – but I had won absolutely nothing. I didn't care about the gym. I didn't care about taking advantage of the manager lady. I didn't even care about the money. What did I care about? I sat there for a while and felt like nothing – nothing. I didn't care about anything. I was empty. There was nothing there. There was no satisfaction for my conquest, so I started to review my other conquests, and it was ditto, ditto, ditto, ditto, ditto.

That was my religious experience. What followed was my eventual reintroduction to someone who stuck out in my mind – someone who I had talked to casually from time to time and even visited. I had some idea that he might know something about what I was going through, and I went to visit him. He didn't live nearby, and I had to travel to South America to see him, but I did it anyway. That's where things began to change for me – from that experience of *winning,* followed by spending a couple of weeks talking to this man. He explained his point of view on the way things are, his interpretation of what had transpired with me, and also what could conceivably evolve from then on. When I returned home, new doors began to open, as old ones began to close. I say began, because it all took a while, and has certainly taken a while since then.

Chapter 16
The Ten Freedoms

The words in this book are for my peers. No, not my peers of age, or gender, or profession, but my peers in what I call "fortunateness" – the millions of people in the western world, and now even elsewhere, who have enough – enough leisure, enough material goods, enough security for the future, enough to eat, enough health, enough options of how to spend their enough leisure.

The basic principle of *fortunateness* is simple. It comes with the recognition that we were placed on Earth for some purpose other than to accumulate more. Once we have accomplished the basics, the ones that not all, but almost all of us already have, another possibility becomes available: the possibility of using one's energy and resources for self-discovery and cheerful selfless service. In fact, this basic principle maintains that peace of mind and fulfillment will only come to us through the pursuit of this *next step*, and all our attempts to avoid it, by regurgitating new and varied reasons to re-accumulate and re-establish our fortunateness, will lead to nothing but frustration and emptiness.

The words in this book are meant to inspire. The inspiration to which I refer is one that is meant to lead toward a new possibility. If you have already discovered that new possibility on your own, and are presently embarked upon it, they are meant to both energize and support you in your new endeavor. Of course for words to be useful they must be read, and for them to be read, potential readers must see them as directed toward answering their questions, and furthering their quest, as they themselves define it.

That necessity for relevancy presented my first obstacle, because most people think that others have enough, but that they themselves need *justalittlemore* to put them in the category of the fortunate. For those of you to whom this applies, I am suggesting an alternate possibility: Whatever loose ends you may see as having to be tied up before you can embark on this new journey, you must reexamine your motivation for increasing your level of fortunateness, because you may already have enough ends tied up. The tying up of those few loose ones may have to be postponed, because even if you happen to accomplish what you think will be this *final tying* in your quest for fortunateness, another loose end will surely loom up behind it. The very fact that you have as many ends tied as you do, may be evidence that you are being called on to take part in a next step – a step of discovery of your true self, and of cheerful selfless service.

Since it is my conviction that coalescing behind a certain unanimity of purpose could help my readers to best absorb and digest these chapters, I want to put forth a description of a particular purpose, in hopes that you could adopt it as your own, at least temporarily as an experiment. The unanimity of purpose to which I refer is the goal of freedom.

The concept of freedom has many interpretations. The most obvious of these is perhaps the political freedoms that we have grown up reading about in history books, and that we see and hear working themselves out on TV and in the news. There are, for example, the freedoms of religion, speech, and movement. There is freedom from oppression, from violence, from discrimination, from disease, from drug and alcohol dependency, from personal physical limitations. Some speak of sexual freedom, others wish for freedom from debt. In the pursuit of many of these freedoms, there is an external, oppressive entity or force that must be either eliminated, reformed, or circumvented.

Though these are of course quite credible freedoms, they are not the freedoms to which this book is addressed. All of my stories and perspectives refer to a category of freedom that could generally be described as freedom from self-destructive attitudes and practices. Since these tendencies are self-generated, they can be removed without the alteration of anyone else's thoughts, feelings, or behavior. Nothing on the part of any other person or entity is required in order to achieve the freedoms that I am addressing. The obstacles to these freedoms are completely self-generated, so they can be completely un-generated.

Some of us formulate our internal aims quite practically – for self-improvement, for example. Some aspire to more esoteric interpretations – religious, spiritual, and transcendent. All these objectives are possible for us, but they are not, at this point, an actuality for us. Something is between our present existence and our finer aspirations.

The place to start in our quest for these freedoms is with ourselves. Not because we are at fault, but simply because involving others can get so damn complicated. We are always with ourselves, so the opportunity to work toward these freedoms is constantly available. Convincing others of anything is often an arduous and potentially exhausting task. Convincing ourselves, I suggest, is a more straightforward, less cumbersome place to begin.

Here is a list of ten freedoms worth seeking. They are all examples of our self-destructive tendencies. They require our attention.

1] Freedom from identification with negative emotions
2] Freedom from a distorted sense of our own importance
3] Freedom from self-deception and dishonesty
4] Freedom from the misconception of responsibility
5] Freedom from fear of other people's opinions
6] Freedom from unexamined concepts
7] Freedom from mechanical behavior
8] Freedom from fear of relinquishing control
9] Freedom from insecurity and material loss
10] Freedom from unconscious imitation

If we can identify, understand, and eventually remove the obstacles to these freedoms, our innate beauty will be revealed beneath them. The stories I have been presenting are geared toward understanding those obstacles and the freedoms they conceal.

So, instead of addressing what we might call the big picture – God realization, enlightenment, and transcendence, I begin with this list of impediments from which we seek freedom. Though these may appear merely to reflect defects in our personality – admittedly a very limited picture – they represent the first obstacles to the Truth, Consciousness, and Bliss to which we all aspire.

It is important for us to understand that the realization of these goals is not just our fancy – it *is* available to us. It *is* a possibility for us. It is in fact the birthright of human beings. It is *our* birthright.

Chapter 17
The Turnaround

When I was seventeen, going to Fort Lauderdale, Florida during Easter break was a pilgrimage. It wasn't a spiritual pilgrimage, but it seemed like one to me at the time. My friends and I would pile into cars and drive the 24-hour ride from New York to Fort Lauderdale in one shot. We had enough drivers to sleep, drive, drive, sleep, stop, eat barbecue, drive, sleep, eat, and get there, alive hopefully. On one of those trips, while we were driving through the necessary succession of states – New Jersey, Maryland, Virginia, North Carolina, South Carolina, Georgia, somewhere in South Carolina we made a gas and bathroom stop. I got out to pee, and didn't realize when I got back in the car that I had left my watch on the sink – a watch that meant a good deal to me. Since I was in somewhat of a stupor, having been sleeping and driving and eating through this 24-hour marathon, it was understandable that halfway through, in the Carolinas, I could space out my watch in the bathroom.

I eventually became aware of what I had done, somewhere in northern Florida or maybe southern Georgia. I looked at my watch to see what time it was, and it wasn't there. I had an extraordinarily alarming feeling – one that everybody is familiar with – that instant of foreboding, because of the possibility of having to turn around and go back the other way. If you're not familiar with that feeling, let me assure you, it is a young person's worst nightmare, because they are always dedicated to going forward.

As we continued driving south, all the while keeping my blunder to myself, I was thinking that maybe I could phone the gas station (if only I could remember the name and find the number). Maybe if I reached them, and the watch wasn't already stolen, I could ask them to hold it for me, and we could pick it up on the return trip home.

Meanwhile, we were adding on miles going south, going in the opposite direction, in the wrong direction to retrieve my watch. I was desperately trying to come up with some way that I could avoid going backwards – anything to avoid turning around and doing the unthinkable – retracing my steps. I remember this because it was such a strong urge and such an unpleasant situation. Here I was, on vacation, in a car with my best friends, riding through different scenery, and I was having a terrible time, because we might have to extend that ride by going backwards.

I'm not going to tell you what I did, because the important point is that I remember the feeling of how much I didn't want to retrace my steps to pick up what I had left behind. I'm telling this story and evoking this feeling in myself, in hopes that you might remember some situation in your own life, when you had this particular experience. If I have not yet succeeded, I have a more exotic turnaround story, or more accurately, a *not* turnaround story, that you might connect with – especially if you are an international traveler or adventurer.

Years ago I spent some extended time in Afghanistan. That was not unusual for me, because I've done a lot of traveling in third world countries, and started doing that when I was relatively young. The hiking on remote trails and driving on terrible roads was very attractive to me, and I've driven in just about every country that I've been to.

The particular trip that I want to tell you about was not war related, or drug dealing related – it was to visit some people who I knew who were living in a remote area of Afghanistan, at the foot of the Hindu Kush Mountains. I was looking forward to spending time with them, especially this one particular man, whose name was Poorhat.

One day, after I'd already been there visiting for a couple of weeks, Poorhat came by to tell me that he needed to go to a village out the Saricha Road to pick someone up and bring them back with us - about a three-day drive each way. That didn't mean it was a great distance, but if you've ever read National Geographic, you know that some of the roads in remote parts of Central Asia are barely roads at all.

He wanted us to drive in my Toyota Land Cruiser – so the next day we took off along a main road to the northeast and then branched off after a while to another road that was going basically straight north toward this village. We drove on that road for the rest of the day till nightfall, when we camped by a river. I don't know the name of that river, but on our second day, the road, which was now dirt, kept along it. It was springtime, and the rivers in Afghanistan, because of the nature of the mountains, get very full, and very flowing, and can be very dangerous.

Eventually, we had to cross this river in the Land Cruiser, and we came to a place where there was a bridge. Most bridges in this area are mediocre, but generally adequate, and if you check them out before you cross, they're relatively safe, even in high water times. The dirt road on the far side of the river was very bad, but it was the only one that led to the village we were heading to. We had to cross, because the road we were riding on was on the west side of the river, and the village was on the east side of the river. So even though we were still a day away from where we were going, at some point we had to cross the river, and here was a place to do it.

The downside of crossing this bridge was that if we crossed now, we would have to ride up the east road, which was a very poor dirt road cut into the side of a mountain. Also, it was very narrow, so it was one way north on some days, and the other way south on other days, and we weren't sure which day we were on. Before we crossed, we decided to ask some people on the west side of the river if there were a crossing further up, maybe even at our destination.

As anyone who's traveled in third world countries knows, whatever you ask of a local, the answer is always "yes" – so the credibility of local people is always questionable, because people want to be nice and positive. They're okay to tell you it's dangerous, and you're going to die if you go there (usually places they haven't been), but if the answer to your question requires a yes or no – they'll tell you "yes." People were telling us that we shouldn't cross yet, because there was a bridge right at the town, and we wouldn't have to take the narrow dirt road up the other side of the mountain, which was very dangerous.

So we stayed off the bridge, traveled on our side of the river for another day, and eventually got to the west side of the village. Voilà! There was no bridge, and the river was flowing fiercely. It was obvious that there *had* been a bridge, but only its remnants were visible. The village was on the other side of the river, and there were a few houses on the west side of the river where we were. Unfortunately, the person who we were there to pick up, didn't live in one of them.

There was no way to cross the river at that point. So once again, I had to relive the *leaving the watch behind* moment, because the only way to get to the village was to travel back on that road a whole day, cross the river, and go up the other road. That was it. Now Poorhat, who I was traveling with, and who was a good deal older than I, and also privy to a lot more wisdom than I, said, "That's no problem, we'll have more time to be together," but of course for me it was a problem. *Oh my God! Drive all the way back there, cross the bridge, go back to the other side, two more days on the road!*

There were people living in a dozen shacks and huts on the west side of the river where we were. They weren't living in the town, and didn't have stores or access to the town or anyplace to get anything.

I remember the next few moments as clearly as I remember not wanting to go back for the watch. I asked Poorhat why anybody would live there, instead of going to the village, and he said, "Those are the people who wouldn't turn around."

If it weren't for Poorhat, I would have been one of those people who wouldn't turn around. I might have set up a life on the west side of the river. But since I was with Poorhat, we did go back to the bridge, crossed, drove up the narrow one-way road, and got to the village a couple of days later. We completed our mission, and I don't remember anything unpleasant about that extra journey.

What I do remember is the lesson I learned and re-learned – *sometimes going back is indicated.* Everything that we've been taught in life accentuates that repetition is the enemy, and should be minimized, and that going back is only necessary if all else fails. Contrary to that point of view, sometimes going back is indicated, though we might have to struggle with what we've learned, and how we've been programed, and what our attitudes are about going back. Sometime we might have to do that, even though there might be no lost watch, and no raging river. This time might be one of those times for you. I'm going to try to explain why.

All of you have been exposed to ideas of spiritual evolvement, of some ascending to a state that is more peaceful, more inner-directed, less reactive – a state that allows more for compassion than for greed – a state that lends itself more to your being here now, rather than in the future or in the past. All of you have read about and been subjected to ideas of this kind. Even though there are so many other demands and attractions that the world produces for us, there are some people who are still curious about this possibility for themselves. This curiosity can lead a person to take a workshop, or read a certain book, or go to a meeting, or experiment with some practice or discipline on their own.

Sometime in that process, a person will likely cross paths with the idea of meditation. Meditation is put forth as some seed process that can lead to inner harmony, quietness of the mind, a finer more elevated state of being. So we hear about this idea of meditation, and wonder, *where can this activity called meditation be learned?* Eventually, if we are even mildly persevering, we'll meet someone who will introduce us to a practice that they call meditation of some kind.

What you don't understand is, though meditation actually is a doorway to the unknown, a doorway to those inner experiences of harmony that you seek, meditation is an extremely advanced part of the process of realizing freedom. There are preliminary steps that must be taken – steps that you might consider to be going backwards – steps that you imagine you've already taken. You would strongly prefer not to retrace your steps, but before you know the inner reality, you have to know the outer reality.

The onion can only be peeled from the outside, layer by layer. You have to know yourself impartially, or know your selves impartially, which is even more subtle. If your life is full of negative emotions, then that must be addressed, because negativity is much too coarse for a meeting with meditation. If you are too goal oriented, that would also be a problem. Bringing that attitude to meditation is definitely counter-productive. So you see, there is much to do before a person can begin to actually meditate.

The dread of having to go back is one that I thoroughly and absolutely sympathize with, because hey man, I've been there. I've been on the west side of that river. I've been on Highway 301 going south from New York to Florida. I know how it feels to think you were going forward, but find out that maybe you gotta go back first. But if you do – you do.

Chapter 18

A New Hand

This is my fourth book. *Another Heart in His Hand* was my first, and I wrote it about twenty years ago. It was about two poker players who met, and had some interesting adventures and conversations. When a book has been published and is in the bookstores, if an author wants people to read that book, they have to promote it. After the first few book signings, I realized I didn't like both the formality, and the lack of originality of the dynamic, so we came up with a different idea. I would do something like a one-man show to promote the book.

I was living in Arkansas, so we tried out that concept in small venues in nearby St. Louis and Dallas, and each time I came up with a different creative way of presenting myself. It was interesting and fun, and certainly different for the people who attended. Eventually we set one up in Hollywood, even though I wasn't living in California at the time. Since the book involved two poker players, I decided to do a card trick in that show. I chose a guy from the audience to stand up on the stage with me and put the deck in his pocket. Then I asked questions of different people in the audience in order to come up with one card. Everybody agreed that the card should be the eight of diamonds. Then I told the guy who had been standing next to me, to pick a card out of his pocket without looking, because the deck of cards had been in his pocket the whole time. So he picked out a card and it was the seven of diamonds. He held it up and showed it to the audience. They were aghast, and probably embarrassed for me, because when you see somebody on a stage do a card trick, you expect that it's going to come out right. But I didn't want it to come out right, I wanted it to come out *close*. So that made it a really magnificent card trick.

Of all the things I did to promote the book – the shows, the radio and TV interviews, the newspaper interviews – that card trick was my favorite one. I got to use a deck of cards to present the idea that coming in second is a disappointment, and even an embarrassment, even though only one person in a hundred or more might come in second. There are fifty-two cards in a deck, and the seven of diamonds is only one card away from the eight, but sadly, it's not close enough to be a recognizable accomplishment. The silver medal is something to be ashamed of, or at least not proud of.

I also got to talk about the game of poker, in which every hand that's dealt is a new opportunity. The continuity that we imagine doesn't really exist, because in life, each moment of each day, the cards come back, they get shuffled and we have a new hand. But our feeling is that continuity is necessary, that we have to keep it going as it was. The only thing that actually has continuity, is we have the same body tomorrow as we do today. A little more decomposed, but basically the same body. But the necessity that we feel for projecting our thoughts and feelings into the next day, into the future, is something that we ourselves develop. So when we see someone tomorrow that we've seen today, we relate to that person in the same way as we did yesterday – it's not a new day; it's a continuity connecting the past day with the present day, with the future day, completely created by us.

I'm not saying this is bad or good, but it is completely created by us, and yes, it is sometimes necessary. That this was your house yesterday, and it's your house today is something you perpetuate. If *you* don't recognize it, if *you* don't remind yourself of that, it will no longer be the place you go home to. It's the same with any attitude you have. It's something that you have to maintain and re-create. We feel good doing that, especially when it's part of a winning hand.

But in actuality, what we think is happening is not happening. We're feeling the pressure of that repetition, but what's happening is in each moment the cards are coming back, and being re-dealt, the cards are coming back, and being re-dealt, the cards are coming back, and being re-dealt. But when we get a hand that we like being part of, we want to project it into the next moment, into the next moment, into the next moment.

So we try to find a profession for ourselves, an image for ourselves, where there will be a continuity – so that what we like about this hand we've been dealt now, we can have tomorrow. We have no idea how much the driving force in our lives is to find a place to hide – to find a place that is one of those good hands that we were part of, that we're trying to re-create in the present now, in each next moment, even though we're being dealt another hand. That hand lasted a moment, and now another hand, and now another hand, and now another hand, but we're always looking for a place to hide by pretending there is continuity. Even people who have been dealt terrible hands, cleave to continuity by feeling self-pity, and losing hope that tomorrow could be different.

It's understandable; this is a very big world. We're very small, it's very big. It lasts a long time, we last a short time. It's understandable that we are looking for some safety, we're looking for some consistency. But at what point does that safety in continuity become self-destructive, and in fact preclude us from having an experience we would never otherwise have? What if that search for safety, limits us from discovering the greatest mysteries of existence and creation? That would probably be more safety than we would wish to have. But we have become machines for seeking safety; we're always picking up our bags and looking for a place to hide.

People choose to hide in the strangest places. There are innumerable personal styles, so there are innumerable ways to hide. People can be on a stage and entertaining thousands of people. It may look to us like that's no place to hide, but for that person, it's the best place to hide. Put that person in another circumstance, and they will feel ill at ease, or they will feel the necessity to somehow alter that situation, so that it is a satisfactory place for them to hide.

A few people hide as acrobats swinging back and forth in Cirque du Soleil. A few people hide behind their appearance. A few people hide by making sure there are non-stop activities happening around them. A few people hide in solitude. A few people hide by having their closest relationships be with animals. A few people even hide by having their best relationships be with inanimate objects, like cars. But *everyone* hides by maintaining the illusion that life is not a sequence of moments, ignoring that the next hand is always in the process of being dealt.

What are the dangers of safety, and what are its limitations? Are we precluding ourselves, not from the American dream, but from the human dream? There is a human possibility of discovering life's greatest mysteries. What if we knew that we were excluding ourselves from those realizations by overdoing our hiding in search of safety? Then we very well might reconsider, not all of our moments, and not the entire diorama of our life, but the times when we felt somewhat disquieted by our circumstances, and immediately thought *something has to be done to quell this feeling of not knowing exactly what's happening in this moment.* We might reconsider, if we understood that the opposite of safety is adventure.

I recently have been reading a book about Roy Chapman Andrews. He was a naturalist and an adventurer who worked for the New York Museum of Natural History. He was sent all over the world to collect fossils. He lived in the early 1900s, and did research on the origins of man, and the origins of plant and animal life. He never stood still. He was a perpetual adventurer, always seeking his next exploit in the Arctic, in Mongolia, in China. He was always on the move, always looking for something new.

That was his place to hide, because when he had to sit still, he was not okay. That was the part of adventure he wasn't interested in. He thought he had to go to wild and exotic places to find adventure. What he had understood correctly, was that we are natural adventurers. What he had failed to understand, was that our ultimate quest is our internal one. He never came to *that* adventure. He only had a sequence of more and more and more exciting external adventures.

We must correctly begin with being external adventurers, because there is no way that we can pursue the internal adventure, if we are not also external adventurers. Our life is thrust out externally from the time we are children. We're curious, and we want go places, and to know things. Then, unfortunately, we hear some words, either on the tube or on the web, or in person, and we get subdued. "It's impossible, you can't do that, it's too far away, it's not practical." We are told these things, and end up following some other road in quest of safety, rather than adventure.

But then hopefully, at some point, we see that our safe road has been repetitious, or boring, or dry, and we feel the pull toward external adventure. It's essential to feel that pull. There's something magnificent in feeling that human life is a quest that has to be sought after. If you either have been subdued into denying your adventure, or you never had an idea of one in the first place, then it may be time that you rediscover and pursue some adventure that calls out to you. It is not possible that you could become an adventurer into the world of consciousness, if you don't first begin in the world of ordinary possibilities.

Chapter 19
Too Personal a Tale

I heard a story about a letter that the author Laurens Van der Post received. He's someone who is not known very well in our country. He grew up in South Africa, and wrote books about his life there. One is called *Story Like the Wind* and the sequel is called *A Far Off Place.* They are in sequence, and several of the characters starts off as children living on an African farm, and after some revolutionary turmoil, they take off with their dog and go on a journey.

The story is beautifully written and very detailed – the kind of book you can really get immersed in – not like getting involved in a movie that lasts two hours, or like Chinese food – after a while you need more. Sometimes, when you've taken a couple of months of your life to read a long book, where the story is very involved and personal, and the characters are interesting, you get attached to those stories, and to those people.

So somebody wrote a letter to Laurens Van der Post, and asked, "I just finished *A Far Off Place,* and I read *Story Like the Wind,* and I want to know if Francois and Nonni ever got together?" It's an understandable question, because this person spent a couple of months of their life with these fictional characters, and they're really invested in them. Then the book ends, and what do you do? Who do you ask about something that takes place after the book ends? You can't ask your neighbors or your friends, so you go to the only place you can go – to the author. "Please tell me what happened with these people. I really want to know." That's pretty funny, even interesting, but in a way it's not so different from our lives.

If there were an encapsulated description of one category of freedom, it would be: *to have the awareness of the subjectivity of our stories*. Our personal stories are not objective realities. They are subjective constructs of which we are a part.

I know a guy who has, what you'd call, delusions. He thinks there are mountain lions living with him. He has this story, and it's very developed for him. They have colors, and textures, and names – he thinks and feels he knows these mountain lions. We would call that behavior insane, but only because his story is not widely held, and defies the senses. We cannot see those mountain lions, only he can see them.

If this guy who sees mountain lions would meet you on the street and say, "Hello, how are you doing? Listen I have a question. I'm really tied up with this problem – what should I feed my lions?" You'd say . . . what would you say? What could you say? It's his reality, it's not your reality, and he's asking you to involve yourself in a conversation about feeding mountain lions.

How about our stories? If our reality and our stories are about our problems, plans, and relationship issues, we will also look to resolve those things by thinking about them and talking about them. So when one person says to another, "I have this problem. I've been living with this person, and I'm just tired of it. What do you suggest?" That sentiment is commonly held. It doesn't defy the senses, it's not insane.

But does that mean that one person can actually respond to another, when it's not their reality also? Is it possible that one person can converse with another, without them both having the same reality? If it weren't their reality, would it be like hearing about feeding mountain lions? Is there a possibility that when two people *do* share the same constructed subjective reality, the more they talk about, and discuss, and question, and answer these constructs, the more real they become, and no longer appear subjective?

So we talk about our problems ad nauseam, and they become real. We talk about our likes and dislikes ad nauseam, and they become real. They don't remain a story, like a Laurens Van der Post story, because the more we involve ourselves in juggling these things that we consider to be realities, the more they appear to become objective realities.

If there were a possibility of realizing the one reality – not the external reality, not the constructed reality, but a reality from which everything else descended – one that was there in the beginning, it would be necessary to begin on that journey of realization by understanding the subjectivity of the stories that we call our lives.

Chapter 20

The Boomerang

When we are born, we are flung out into life. It's appropriate that we be flung out. We are born into a world that we are meant to explore. We're born with all the equipment needed to do that. That's why we have that equipment. That's why we have our senses. We explore with our senses: *What does this feel like, and taste like, and smell like? What does this look like? Let me have some of that, let me try some of that.*

This is as it should be. All of us have to embrace and taste this world. As we explore and embrace the world, we begin to develop a platform that can more successfully do that. Some of us have been more effective in that quest. Those of us who proceeded boldly have accelerated the pace of this exploration, as compared to those of us who are timid.

However this phase of human life has gone, or is going for a person, they will have to contend with the fact that there are an almost infinite number of permutations of experience, in our affluent and flexible culture. Regardless of how many external experiences a person has, there will always be a potential tweak to that experience that will make it appear as new. There is almost no limit to the exploration of the senses, and many people never pass to the next phase, because of the appearance of originality. Without personal honesty, or at least paying attention, a person could claim newness in any endeavor, whether it be a relationship, a business, or a hobby, by merely changing the venue of that activity.

At some point, after a good deal of this going out in exploration, if we're paying attention, and are somewhat honest with ourselves, our lives can begin to feel repetitious. We come to suspect that the next repetition will be just another variation on a theme that we have already lived. We suspect that because we've explored; we've lived in some different places, and tried some different things.

We want something more – we feel there must be something more – something different. We suspect that there is some elusive depth of quality, that there is some other direction. That suspecting is indicative of a slowing down of one phase, and an entering of another. You know the way it is with a boomerang. It goes out, it goes out, and out, and at some point before it turns for home, it's absolutely standing still, right? At some point it has gone out as far as it's going to go, and now it's going to be coming back.

Certainly when you're a teenager, you should feel enthusiasm for your next hope, your next project, whatever this next thing is that's going to do it for you. But after years of repetition and repetition, you start to feel a little, what you might call, *burnt out*. If that experience is a product of your having explored, *burnt out* is a very good place, a very healthy place. Now you're suspecting something else is called for, and maybe it's time to head toward home. Not instantly come home, but to turn around, turn around, face in a different direction – an internal direction.

We want to begin on that return journey, but what about all the equipment that we used on the going out? It was so effective for us, it protected us – after all, we're here, we're alive. Can we keep that paraphernalia intact and remaining with us? When rocket ships are sent up, they have certain equipment, but when they're coming back they have to let go of that equipment – stage one, stage two, stage three. In this new stage, some of that gear is not going to serve you.

As you approach the outer turn of your boomerang curve, you still need much of your old equipment. Certainly you need your old personality and your self-image. You need to continue to protect yourself in old ways, because you're only beginning to turn for home. But as you continue your turn toward home, you find a new kind of support – one that is different from your old safety net.

With that new support, you can be more as you are, and it's okay. You don't have to pretend as much. As you get nearer to home, you can actually relax, because you're becoming aware of the energy that keeps you alive. You're starting to get filled up from within, so you don't have to fill yourself up from without. As you make that turn and begin to face home, you need less and less of those protective devices. There's nothing that you need protection from.

It can sound threatening to have to begin to let go of your cleverness, or other qualities that have helped you to stand out. Your particular claims to fame and to personal significance – they were all so helpful to you. Those protections were essential, and important, and supplied a feeling of self-worth that was required on the way out!

The return trajectory of this boomerang is not a lightning bolt. It's a gradual slowing down. You find yourself keeping many of your old attitudes, but decreasing, decreasing – not because they're taken from you, not because you're losing them, but because in your reexamination, you see that you don't need them anymore. You don't need your doubt, and your cynicism, and your anger, and your self-righteous indignation, or your self-pity. You don't need those anymore.

They were very important when you were competing. How could you have succeeded without them? How could you have given your best unless people were shouting, "Okay, go for it! Way to go!" You know the way it happens in team sports. How else could you have given your best? People love to play on their home court because the crowd is shouting. Every team waits to get on its home court. If you bet on a sports match, the home team is always favored by a few points. Why? The court is exactly the same, the measurements are the same, but the rooting section is not.

On the way *out*, people do better when others are cheering for them. But on the way *home*, you do your best, because it's the natural thing to do. You don't need people to notice it. You can give up the need for recognition that was so important on the way out.

Maybe you're ready to make the turn for home. Maybe not quite yet. Maybe you have more business to take care of, but you're slowing down a little. If that weren't the case, you wouldn't still be reading, you'd be out selling, either something or yourself.

Some of us are recognizing that attitudes we were sure we needed, can be let go of a little. In letting go of some of those weights that were so important to us as part of the competitive phase of life, our state of being naturally rises. We find ourselves a little kinder, a little bit more patient, a little bit more understanding. Did we study kindness, patience, and understanding? No. It went with the territory of a raised state of being. We can listen a little better, we can sit still a little longer, we can receive a little better. We're a little more curious about something that may not have anything to do with our personal aggrandizement. We're a little less confident in our opinions, because we know the opposite view also has substance. Those qualities begin to come naturally, not without labor, but naturally. Our effort as we start to return, is to notice what's weighing us down, to be open to the new idea that what we considered of value to us before, upon re-examination may not be of value any more.

I used to live in Santa Barbara, California. The Pacific Ocean there is always relatively cold. In winter it's very cold, in summer, it's still cold. I learned to windsurf when I lived there, so I got used to wearing a wetsuit – they warm you up. When I took a windsurfing trip to Aruba, I of course took my wetsuit with me. I learned in it. I have to wear it. I've always worn it – that's the way it is. In Aruba I put it on, and noticed that other people weren't wearing wetsuits.

After a while I decided to take a chance and take it off. "But no," I thought, "I won't take it off, I'll get a shorty. Yes, I'll cut the legs off. I'll try that." Eventually I was without a wetsuit. Why? Because it was taken away from me? Would you think, "I lost my wetsuit?" No, you wouldn't think that at all. You would think, "I don't need it here. It weighs me down. It never was that much fun to put it on anyway. It was necessary, so I did it because I like to windsurf, but I don't need it now."

On the way home, you notice that there are things you needed before, that you don't need anymore. You examine, you study, you explore, you see what you don't need, and you take it off. No one is taking anything away from you. No one wants to take anything away from you. Your decisions are based on your personal understanding, your personal wisdom, your personal ability to assess your situation as it is now, and your observation of what is extra, and the knowledge that whatever is extra is weighing you down.

Chapter 21
Galileo

I have always been curious about astronomy. How could one not be? There's so much out there. In comparison to what would be possible to know about that subject, I know very little, and before I studied it a bit, I knew much less – maybe only the names of the planets. I was curious enough about astronomy, that some years ago, I decided to buy a telescope. I could afford to buy something other than a toy, and had once met someone who let me look through his 8 inch, Schmidt-Cassegrain, which is one of those stubby ones that real astronomers use. Other than that, my only context for telescopes, was the huge ones that stick out of domes, and I knew I wouldn't be able to afford one of those.

So I bought a really good used one that had a spotting scope, and equipment to take photographs. I was going to have to learn how to use all of it from scratch. This telescope had an electric plug. I didn't know why you would plug in a telescope, and there was nothing in the instructions to say why you would plug one in. But there was a plug, and I had an outlet. I was in a cabin, and it was very dark – the circumstances were perfect for stargazing, so I plugged in the telescope and tried to see something through it. Plugging it in didn't seem to do anything, and that first time I had very little success in seeing much, but it was fun playing with my new telescope anyway.

The next morning when I woke up, the telescope was pointing into the floor. I thought it had broken, but I eventually discovered that the electricity actually operated a rotating mechanism which followed the movement of the earth and stars. You could actually track something at the speed of the earth's rotation. I had no idea that telescopes moved. After playing with it for a while, I realized I was going to have to learn a bit about astronomy before I actually could make use of my new acquisition. So I put some energy into learning the basics, and even read some about the history of astronomy. I remember facts to this day about that subject. Here are some of those facts that still interest me.

Aristotle, who we know as a philosopher, also had theories about the configuration of the universe. His theory was that the earth was the center of it all. Aristotle saw the Earth as unmoving and in the center. He deduced this partly because, if the Earth was moving, then we'd feel it. Also, if the Earth was moving, the birds and the clouds would get left behind as it moved. So he deduced that the Earth was stationary, and the center of the universe. Ptolemy further defined his theory from Aristotle's ideas and from some of his own – that the Earth is the center of the universe, which we of course know it isn't . . . *we are!*

This theory was supported for 1,500 years. That is quite a long time. The theory of an unmoving perfect Earth being the center of everything supported the dogma of the Catholic Church, so they were behind it, and the Church was very powerful during those 1,500 years.

That theory remained relatively unchallenged up until the time of Copernicus. His calculations produced evidence that the previous theory was flawed. Copernicus produced a theory that the Sun was actually the center of the universe – not only the center of the solar system, but the center of the universe. He couldn't really prove it, because he didn't have the equipment. He had the mathematics to prove it, but Galileo, who came shortly thereafter in the 1600s, developed the telescope, and was confident that he had proven that the Sun was the center of the Universe, and the planets went around the sun, and the Earth rotated on its own axis.

Sometime after that, our galaxy, the Milky Way, was discovered, and it became evident that our solar system wasn't even in the center of that galaxy. Astronomers went on to discover that there is an almost infinite number of galaxies in what we call the Universe, and that the Earth is a grain of sand on the beach of infinity in relation to that vastness.

In each case, when these theories were agreed upon, the ideas derived from those theories were acknowledged as facts. There were serious consequences for those who challenged the existing theory, starting from Aristotle, Ptolemy, Copernicus, Galileo, and the Catholic Church. Those theories, once they were agreed upon, gave comfort. *Okay, that's the way it is. I can rest easy, because I know the way it is.*

Once those theories were challenged, that comfort, that satisfaction, that security of knowing, or thinking one knew how it was, was disrupted. Those challenges caused trouble. There were people who even went to prison, and were burned at the stake because of challenges to those theories. They prompted the need to reexamine, and when someone feels they have a hold of something that is a fixed point, reexamination is a challenge. Challenges are always a challenge, so each time there were changes in astronomical theory, there was tremendous resistance. So we know something about human nature, which hasn't changed. *Reexamination is a challenge, and it will be accompanied by resistance.*

As we know now, there are more educated views on what actually is. Not only is the Earth not the center of the universe, but there are contemporary discoveries in many areas other than astronomy, that require us to reexamine how those new findings alter our previous perception. Cultural anthropology is one of those areas.

Harp seals give birth to their young, and desert them shortly thereafter – not through negligence or self-interest, but through a genetic stamp that guides their actions. Elephants give birth to their offspring, and stay with some of them in a family group for the rest of their lives, also not because of personal dedication or morality, but dictated by a different genetic stamp. That is a huge continuum of behavior.

A few years ago I was in Costa Rica, and went to a place called Tortuguero, on the northeast coast in a fairly dense jungle area. The only way to get there was by boat. There are no roads up there, so you get somebody who has a boat, and they, in true third world manner, drive you up river for four hours with as much speed and noise as a double outboard motor can deliver. When we got up there, we stayed in some broken down old military barracks that were deserted.

The draw of this place is the turtles; the beach is a turtle sanctuary for humongous turtles that are laying their eggs – and people get to watch. Thinking about watching turtles lay eggs just didn't do it for me, but you know, when you’ve come this far, etc., etc., etc.

I was with my son Adam, when the ranger came around to our cabin at 4 am. He shined the flashlight on us, telling us it was time to go see the turtles laying eggs. I looked at Adam, and he looked at me, and we both had similar reactions, but we knew we had to go. We went out to the beach looking for these turtle eggs, which are quite large – about like tennis balls. The ranger is setting us up for a disappointment, in case it might not work out. "We don't always find turtle eggs, and we don't always see the turtles.”

It's pitch dark and there’s no moon, and he's telling the story of the turtles, and I'm not getting anything out of it. We're walking on the sand, so at least we can't trip on anything, unless it happens to be a 700 lb. tortoise. He says, "There's tracks, there are the tracks!" He points his flashlight, and there are tracks in the sand where turtle fins had been scraping along the ground – and then we see a big, I mean *big* tortoise.

I guess they're either used to people, or they can't move too fast anyway. Their protection is their shell. Then the ranger starts scraping in the sand underneath the bottom of the tortoise, where the tortoise lays her eggs. That looked really offensive, if you can relate it to anything personal. He's kicking sand and digging, and the tortoise is trying to get her eggs laid, but she's going about it anyway. He shines his flashlight where this tortoise is laying the eggs, and we're watching them drop out of the tortoise's bottom, and then the tortoise swishes her fins and covers up the eggs. People are standing around *ooooh-ing and ahhh-ing*, probably because they got up at 4 am, and traveled a long distance to get to Tortuguero. I guess they had to *ooooh, ahhh.* I didn't really get it, but something about what I observed did interest me.

I sat down on the sand there, and after watching three or four eggs drop, I looked up at the stars, and out at the white waves of the ocean, which were only about 50 ft. away. It was a very wonderful place to be, very warm and jungly, even in the middle of the night.

After the turtle flaps around covering the egg spot so it’s level with the sand, it does something unbelievable, at least from my perspective. It leaves, never to return. Maybe that's what I came there to see, because the dropping wasn't so consequential to me. It really struck me – that this great big being could actually give birth and then flop away, knowing it would never return. I imagine, in some way, it also cognized the rest of the process. These baby turtles would hatch themselves, run to the ocean, the birds would pick off 99% of them, and 1% would make it to the ocean to increase the tortoise population.

Moving on from turtles to human beings, considering the rest of our state-of-the-art equipment being what it is, would we have been denied a genetic guidepost of our own in this matter? If we have one, has it been lost, or at least so covered up that we have no idea what our natural obligation is to our offspring? Human beings have exhibited examples of the entire spectrum of behavior, between harp seals and elephants. Certainly more of the second than the first, but the subject remains a lifelong confusion for those of us who have spawned.

Reexamination is why I wrote this book, and hopefully why you're reading it – not to compound what you already know, because what you already know has delivered you to who you are now. If you're not satisfied with that, and if you don't have the experience of life you think is possible, then something else has to be explored. If your conclusions to this point, your knowledge to this point, your experience to this point, have not led you to understanding, and to calm, and to compassion – then some reexamination may be in order.

As we have learned, new explorations are a challenge, and challenges are always accompanied by some amount of resistance. If one imagines that resistance is not going to appear, the process of reexamination is going to come to a point when a person will abort. Awareness that resistance will come in some form, can help keep a person stay on the path to new discoveries – and yes, of course – knowing like-minded allies is also a must.

Chapter 22
The Racetrack

As a young man I was very involved in the gambling business – not that I was a gambler, which I looked on as being beneath me, but that I was an entrepreneur. It was something that meant a lot to me. It was my passion. Specifically, this involved running poker games as well as spending a lot of time at the racetrack. I started working out racehorses when I was about nineteen, and later went on to get involved with the stables, and eventually booking bets on horses. It was very exciting and had a very strong pull on me. I loved it – not only the horses; I loved the action. You know "the action"? It was the opportunity never to have to stop, or even slow down. That was very attractive to me at the time. This particular vocation kept me going for a while, and I was financially successful at it.

Eventually, I got involved in activities at the track that were quasi-legal: selling inside information gleaned from horse owners and trainers, and cashing very large winning race tickets for people who wanted to avoid having to give their Social Security number for tax purposes. There were no laws against what I was doing, but it did conflict with the rules of the racetrack. If you're involved in questionable activities, as careful as you are, sooner or later somebody who's watching will see them.

I went to the racetrack every day. My friends were there, I was well regarded there, and it was exotic and exiting. It was the place I felt most at home. Eventually, because of these questionable activities, I was put on the known gambler list, known as the KG list. This didn't have much impact on me at first, other than that I had to watch my step, but after a few months, I was barred from the racetrack.

This was one of the most confronting things that had happened to me up to that point in my life. It was like being kicked out of your house when you aren't ready to leave home yet. I had no idea how to handle it. Was I going to put on disguises? Was I going to sneak in through some service entrance where they didn't have my picture posted on the KG list? Would I go to other cities and other racetracks – or what?

I really didn't know the answer, but I was very upset. This activity that meant so much to me was being withdrawn, and I had no say in it. It was not within my control to alter matters. These were very heavy times for me. I went from, "This may be over," to, "It's probably over," to, "It looks like it's over," to, "From the evidence it appears very strongly that it's over." Whatever I thought – it was over. I just had to come to grips with it.

Eventually I gave up the hope of returning to the racetrack. I quit the gambling business, left New York, and never returned. Circumstances helped me to recognize that I just had to let go. Needless to say, my life has changed significantly from those days. It wasn't easy to let go, but sometimes the message is clear, and you have to listen to it. *This is over. Just let go*. Like when you have a relationship, or a job, and you really know it's just over, but you hang on, and it hurts. Hanging on hurts, especially when something is changing – hanging on hurts.

I know we're supposed to be able to leave the past behind. We've all read about it in some book or other. But it's not so easy when some thing or person or situation that we've depended on has been withdrawn from us. We've all known, or know about, people who have had physical beauty in youth, and then they get older. It's impossible to retain that same physical beauty, but sometimes you see a person trying to. It looks so desperate – it's painful, and they suffer. Clearly the later time of life is for something other than attracting people with your physical appearance, but that person hasn't learned that. It's just like I hadn't learned to depend on anything except the racetrack, and when they said the gates were closed, I suffered.

Remember when hitchhiking was so easy? Now hitchhiking is over. Maybe it will come back, but for now it's over. You ex-hitchhikers don't even pick up people anymore. So it's over. How about the people who are still trying to hitchhike? They're not having a good experience. They're cursing three times as many people. It's painful. When you hold on to something that's ending, it's painful.

Learning to let go, or at least loosen up, is so important in work on consciousness. If we're brought together by our inner purpose, by something that draws us – this something is going to cause changes to happen. You should be aware, that in direct proportion to your proximity to the flame of this work – some of your old doors will begin to close for you. They won't abruptly slam shut, but they will begin to close, as other doors will begin to open. The doors that open are sometimes intimidating but generally attractive. The doors that close are often scary. That's something that we have to recognize and support each other in, because those changes will happen.

I'm not talking about changes that come because the New York State Racing Association says to me, "You can't do this anymore," or that the nature of people's lives become so separate, that hitchhiking is not going to happen anymore. I'm also not talking about changes that come through some retrograde force, but rather through the force of the evolution of consciousness. This force can be very defined when someone puts their energy toward experiencing that evolution. It does bring about changes, but not through somebody telling you to change.

If you feel the pull to change, and you suspect it's a good change, you should be encouraged to loosen up and go for it. Usually one knows whether a particular change is a good thing or not a good thing. You might be afraid, and try to call it a bad thing, but somewhere in you, you know it's a good thing. If so, it's important to be able to relinquish what you're holding onto as soon as you're ready. If you start feeling pain, you don't have to explain the pain in any other way than *you're holding on*. You're holding on to the hitchhiking. You're holding on to the job. You're holding on to the place you're living. You're holding on to the possession. You're holding on to your appearance. You're holding on to doing it the way you grew up doing it. You're holding on to your secret. You're holding on to your excuse.

You're holding on to something that it may be time to let go of, and it starts to hurt.

The desire to alleviate this pain diverts your spiritual quest into being more anesthetic than esoteric. You want to get rid of the pain from whatever you think is causing you difficulty. You have little energy left to seek deeper meaning in life, to seek progress and expansion. So much energy goes into trying to get relief from difficulty, from pain, from discomfort.

I'm putting forth this formula that we suffer when we hold on – we suffer because something is calling us to change, to relinquish, and we're resisting. We're standing on the road agonizing, but hitchhiking is just over. We're kicked out of the racetrack. We don't look twenty-two anymore. However it is for you, things are changing. Maybe you can start to notice those things that are changing as a joyful possibility, rather than feeling the pain of resistance and constriction and loss.

I'm suggesting the possibility that somewhere in you some good thing is being asked of you, the possibility that some elevating step – not easy, maybe even painful, challenging for sure, but good – is being asked of you from inside yourself, and you're resisting. You're resisting with the demand, "I want it to be the way it was. Hey, it was good for so long. Remember when . . ."

It's not that your glory days are over, but that their medium is going to change – new doors are opening before you. If you're open to this possibility, then your life is going to be remarkable. But if you hold on, it could be tough. It's going to hurt.

Chapter 23

Releasing

A few years ago my friends and I took on a project to renovate a house. We had a few vans between us and some regular cars, but we didn't really have anything to do hauling. We needed a pickup truck. A couple of us went out looking for an old heavy duty truck, so we could hurl construction stuff in it from walls we were breaking down, and not be concerned about it getting dinged. We checked the ads in the paper, and the AutoTrader magazine. The first truck we went to look at was a white dual-wheel pickup. We weren't particularity looking for a dually, but it was nearby, so we decided to look at it.

We went to this person's house, they showed us the truck, and we thought it looked good for our purposes. After taking it for a drive, we asked how much he wanted for it, and he said $7,000. That seemed high, because it was about 15 years old and I had already checked the Blue Book, and it was listed at $5,000. I told him that I liked the truck, but his price sounded a little high, and showed him the Blue Book information.

He responded with a sentence that we've all heard before: "Well that's how much I have into it." He bought the truck, put money into repairs, and he wanted to get that money out, because, *that's how much he had into it*. It didn't matter if it had that value or didn't have that value, that's what he wanted.

That idea interests me. How could this person see the situation clearly, when his concept came from *what he had into it* – what his vested interest in it was? I think it's a very timely subject, both for our world situation, and our spiritual pursuits.

It would be extraordinary if a person in a position of authority could admit they had made a mistake leading us down a road that was not working out. Historically that has been very, very rare. If any of you are students of history, you know that it is very unusual for a political leader to be able to extricate his constituency, or country, from circumstances that he himself has gotten them into. It is very difficult because that person has so much into it.

Everyone knows that the perspective of someone who has a vested interest is hugely different than someone who doesn't. We would like our leaders to be able to admit when they are wrong, and might not have a clue what to do, but they can't, because they have so much into the course of action they have been taking. They want to get back what they have into it, and that eliminates any chance of flexibility.

Now let's get to the relevant subject – our lives. Think of a person admitting that about their life. They have failed to find peace. They have failed to be compassionate.

They have been able to take love, but they have failed to give love. They have failed to find the connection to their inner truth. But can they acknowledge what they want somebody else to acknowledge? *Well, I've led myself down the wrong path. I've made some mistakes, but I'm locked in right now. I'm not the right person to make the next decision, because I have a vested interest in trying to vindicate my past actions – I have a lot into it.*

Here's an interesting example. As a kid I was a big canoeing enthusiast. Every year I spent summers on a lake with my family, and after that, as a counselor in summer camps. The water was a big thing for me – swimming and boats, and I had my own canoe. Later I went on canoe trips with the boy scouts – it was something I really liked to do. I remember camping on a sand bar on one trip we took on the Delaware River in Pennsylvania. I had a really fun time on that trip, sleeping out in our sleeping bags on the sand bar. The weather was beautiful, so we didn't have to sleep in tents.

During the night I had a dream that my canoe wasn't pulled up onto the shore correctly, and it floated down stream, which in canoeing circles is about as crude a mistake as you can make. It would be considered a major *faux pas*. I woke up in the middle of the night recognizing clearly that it was a dream, because I saw that my canoe had not sailed down the river. I was in my sleeping bag and everything was fine. As I lay back down and started to fall asleep, the reality in my dream returned, and my canoe was floating down the river again. But this time I wasn't sleeping. I could not dispel the worry, even after I realized the boat wasn't floating down the river.

When I woke up in the morning, I still had some of that anxiety, even though the canoe was right in front of me. I was only a teenager, but still noted, probably for the first time, that there was a problem with the way I functioned as a human being. I could not alter my inner dialogue, even though my reality was right in front of me. Years later, I came to understand the challenge of momentum, and the issue of leaving the past behind, even though we know reasonably that it cannot follow us unless we bring it along. The past has no vehicle with which to follow us, nor is there a trailer hitch up our ass that is hooked to our past. Sometimes, we have so much momentum from the past, that we refuse to let it go.

So how can change really happen? How can a person achieve an elevated state? How can a person leave some of the density behind, and have a loftier experience of life, if we, by our normal and mechanical nature, bring the past along, even though there is no reason whatsoever to do that? Have you ever moved from one city to another, and nobody knows you in this new place? Though no one has a file on your previous behavior, you will, in your first meaningful encounter, tell a person about who you were, not about who you want to be, but who you were. You'll make sure they know who and what you were, even though at that point, you could be somebody new – you could leave everything that weighed you down in your past behind.

A person has to find some way to leave enough of the past behind that they can be receptive to something new coming in. Otherwise it will have the flavor of everything that was before – not a new and different flavor. In order for that to happen, some loosening has to happen. Some alteration of that mechanical pattern has to happen. And it has to happen gently enough that you recognize the transition, gently enough that you are a participant in that process rather than a victim.

Sometimes marijuana can play that part for a person who has not misused it. A person who has used it daily for a way to cope, or to dull the edge of their anxiety, might require something other than a drug. Whatever the catalyst, something is required that can help you to question the necessity of bringing the supports of your past along, even if they no longer apply.

You have stories like, "That's not natural. I want to do it myself. I want to do it without anything interceding, whether it be a person, a place, or a thing. Those are all artificial. I want to do it the natural way. I want to do it myself." The first thing you have to understand, is that if you were natural, then natural would work for you. You may be normal, but you are no longer natural.

There is hardly anything natural about you. The minute a person gets into a car and drives faster than a person can walk, faster than a horse can go, that person becomes a machine operating a machine, and there is nothing natural about going 60 miles an hour. We were not naturally given the capacity to go 60 miles an hour. We were not naturally given the capacity to put a piece of plastic to our ear, and talk to somebody somewhere else who has a piece of plastic to their ear. That is not natural, and we are not natural. So the story that you want to be natural, and you don't want to use anything artificial is ridiculous. The minute you flush a toilet, you become as artificial as the toilet. Those are our conditions, and a substance introduced to us from that artificial world that can actually make possible our journey toward freedom is a gift, not a problem.

Sometimes we have so much invested in our past, that we refuse to part with it or even let it loosen. Not being able to leave self-destructive tendencies from our past behind, is the addiction of which we should be afraid, and for which we should seek help, in whatever form works for us.

As you know by now, I've had exposure to the game of poker for years, ever since I was a kid. Last week I went with some friends to Reno, and I played poker for a while. I don't play often anymore – maybe a few times a year. We got together at night after I played, and somebody asked me if I won – a normal question. I told them I did pretty well. They asked me if I always won, and did I use spiritual powers to figure out what the other players were doing. I told them that would be unethical, but I did have some strengths that are important for being a good poker player.

Do you know what Siddhartha said when he was asked what his strengths were? He said he could *think, wait, and fast*. Well, I can think and wait. Those are definitely two assets that are required in poker. Patience is a very important quality for a poker player, and not getting upset when things don't go your way is another. So we talked about that for a few minutes, and then went on to talk about some other things.

A few days later while driving home in my car, I thought about something else that is an asset in playing poker. There are eight or nine people playing at the table, so it's not expected that you're going to get good cards every time you're dealt a hand. Sometimes you will get something good, and the rest of the time you pretty much have to wait and watch. Also, you may start off with something good, and that something starts to look a little less good, and doesn't materialize like you hoped it would – it happens.

People get married, start a business, travel somewhere, it starts off looking really good – first few cards are great, but then your hand starts to deteriorate. One of the strengths I have, maybe my primary strength, is something in poker called *releasing*. I can give it up, let it go. If it starts off good, and then deteriorates, a lot of people stick with it, in the hope that it is going to turn around, maybe even the miracle card will come that will turn everything around. People frequently lose more than money pursuing hopes that have little or no chance of becoming reality.

I don't think we have to refer to poker anymore, because the strength of being able to leave something behind, to be able to release when you recognize that something is not going to live up to your hopes, is an asset in far more than a card game. That can happen with a talent, that can happen with a relationship, that can happen with a place where you live, and that can with an occupation.

Certainly it is worthwhile to persevere, but at some point, a person can know when there is very little hope. Something new has to be added, something different has to be found, some change has to be made that hasn't been made so far, and something may have to be left behind – released. It certainly is always necessary to release an old idea to adopt a new idea.

I understand that it's challenging to release – it's challenging to let go of even the smallest thing. After all, maybe there is some hope that you can get away with not changing anything. This is our folly – that we can grow in consciousness and keep everything else as it was – that we can add more, and not let go of anything. It's unrealistic in poker, and it's unrealistic in life. Some releasing has to happen. It's really important to understand how reluctant we are to let go of anything that we see as having kept us safe in the past – kept us okay. It is even a challenge for a person to let go of an activity that they have no hope in, but has become a dependable habit. It's even more of a challenge with one's concept of how things are, when that concept was part of your package, part of your equipment – part of what kept you feeling that you knew what was going on. I have sympathy and understanding for how tightly we are wound, however we appear externally.

Maybe it's time to release. Maybe you are on the cusp of a new phase of life, and the command to release is bubbling up from within you. Your past challenges of how to resolve problems, plans, and relationships may be in the process of being replaced by the challenge to discriminate between what needs to be held onto, and what needs to be released.

Chapter 24

Wurtzel the Turtzel

To learn this art of discrimination would seem to take such an unattainably high level of self-knowledge, that it would be almost beyond our reach. And it would be for most of us, were it not for uplifting forces perpetually supporting our efforts. Those forces want us to succeed in our aspirations to be agents of the light, and resisters of the darkness. An experience that I had while still quite young will always be a metaphor for me of this support.

Seven years old may seem young to be getting out on one's own, but in the New York City of the 1950s a kid had to walk to school, and when you walk to school alone, your education begins before the bell rings at 9:00 am, and continues well after 3:00 pm. Until only recently, it had been years since I had been back to my old neighborhood, and the route to PS 114, that in those days mostly passed apartment houses and through parks, was unchanged. There were usually a few stores on the ground floor of some of those residential buildings, but not many. Most of the shopping happened at commercial centers, which were informally located about every six or seven blocks.

I lived on 165th Street, and on 161st Street was our 1950s version of a shopping center – a street lined with stores instead of buildings full of apartments. 161st Street was also the home of the New York Yankees. As I mentioned before, from the roof of my apartment house you could look down into Yankee Stadium. At that time baseball players weren't such celebrities as they are now. Their salaries weren't millions of dollars, so some of the players even lived in my neighborhood, since it was near the stadium.

At any rate, 161st Street wasn't only the home of the Yankees. It was where people went to shop and eat out . . . and of course go to the movies. At seven years old, I wasn't very interested in movies except for Saturday, kids' day, when I was allowed to go by myself. I walked to school alone, and the movies were about the same distance – just in a different direction. For the price of a quarter, my friends and I would sit for most of the day watching cartoons and serials, like Flash Gordon and The Lone Ranger. I wasn't always able to round up the quarter, so I didn't always go, but Wurtzel – we called him Wurtzel the Turtzel – always had his quarter. When you have a last name like that, the other kids usually don't bother with first names.

One Saturday, Wurtzel asked me if I was going to the movies, and I told him that I didn't have a quarter – so he offered to pay for me. In the weeks that followed, sometimes I would have the quarter, and some weeks I wouldn't, but he would always have an extra, so I never had to miss the weekly installment of Flash Gordon – which was mucho important to me at the time. Wurtzel didn't come from a wealthy family, but somehow he always had an extra quarter. Eventually I became interested in what his source was for these quarters, and I asked him how he was able to come up with money every weekend. His answer was spontaneous, simple, and direct. "I take the newspapers down," he said.

Apartment houses in my neighborhood usually had about six floors, and *down* customarily meant the basement – the dark and dulgy catacomb where the coal furnace resided, and the garbage was collected. Nobody would ever want to spend more time down there than absolutely necessary.

When Wurtzel said, "I take the newspapers down," I pictured my basement – a bunch of trash cans lined up in a low-ceilinged concrete room, lit by a bare bulb with a bin alongside that was always full of newspapers – definitely not for recycling. I again asked him how that got him his bottomless stash of quarters. He said, "When the newspapers get to a certain height in my apartment, I take them down, and I get a dollar."

"Hmm," I salivated, as much as a seven-year-old can over money. "That sounds interesting." So being a relatively bright kid, I figured I had a new idea for a source of income. I went back to my apartment, found where the newspapers were stacked, then took them down and dumped them in the bin on top of their predecessors. On my return, I announced to my grandmother, who was in charge of household matters, "I took the newspapers down." She replied something like, "Oh that's great, thanks." I was confused, and since a seven-year-old doesn't debate with a larger-than-life grandmother, who is also the matriarch of the clan – I retired to my room, perplexed.

The next time I saw Wurtzel, I asked him for a few more details, because after doing what I thought *he* did, I didn't get the dollar. I asked if he simply took the newspapers down, or did he sort through them, or were there also magazines which figured into the formula? I was looking for exactly what he did, or maybe some special time that it had to be done. He willingly told me all he could, and eventually I deduced that what I had overlooked had something to do with the time of day this taking down was done.

The next time the newspapers were stacked, once again I picked them up and took them down. I went back to my grandmother with, "I took the newspapers down first thing in the morning, and this time I put them in the bin," I added, to cover another possible base. Again she replied, "Oh that's very good, thanks." I looked and waited but wasn't bold enough to extend my hand for payment – I only waited confused.

I don't remember much more of the story, and I'm probably embellishing the parts that I do recall. But I remember this event making a definite impact on me. I eventually found out that the missing piece was that Wurtzel had an *arrangement* with his parents, and it was this arrangement – not the act of taking down newspapers, that resulted in the reward. His parents *wanted* to give him a dollar, in fact *had* to give him a dollar, to do the things they wanted him to do. But in order for him to get the dollar, they wanted him to do something – something that required putting out some effort. So they came up with a chore that anybody else could have done, and maybe didn't even need being done. He had an arrangement of which I was not aware, and eventually I understood that I didn't have such an arrangement.

I forgot about this lesson for years, until a time much later, when I got involved with a man who had something that I assessed was important for me to acquire. This time it wasn't money. It was some knowledge, some wisdom, some information, some methods. I remembered back to Wurtzel and my dulgy basement, so I was a little bit ahead of the game, because I already understood something that appeared to run parallel to the newspaper affair.

This man wanted to give me what he had. He wanted me to have it – but in his judgment, in order for me to get it, and make use of it, and appreciate his wisdom and methods, he was going to ask me to do something. So my appraisal of the situation, which ordinarily would have been that it all depended on my performance, was altered.

I understood that in actuality, the most important element was that this man, who was in possession of some extraordinary wisdom, wanted to share it with me. Even though he introduced my part of the contract as supremely important, he did not put it forth any more importantly than Wurtzel's parents presented his to him. Probably they told him that he was playing his part in the family, and was taking the burden off somebody else, etc., so that he would be getting a dollar for doing it.

This is a critically misunderstood point, and the better we understand it, the better will be our chances of reaching our pursuit of something higher – true love, awakened consciousness, or however we define our goal. There is an importance to our personal efforts, but the confusion of their relative consequence has led people to feel frustrated, to feel self-important, self-indulgent, and introspective in a self-defeating way. This misunderstanding to which I refer, leads to these pitfalls, and since it may be possible to circumvent, it is well worth the discussion.

Some of you have already made deliberate efforts toward awakening, and some of you have not yet felt or acted on that impulse. But for everyone, it is either important to know this in the first place, or be reminded about it before it has become a problem. *As necessary as our efforts are, they are not the most important thing*. The most important thing, is that they are solicited from a place that wants us to succeed, so the efforts that we are asked to make are not an adversity. Our efforts are only the part that we're asked to play in this game of life. The more sincerely we play, the more consistently, heartfelt, and conscientiously we respond, the more we are fulfilling our part of the arrangement.

If Wurtzel's parents couldn't give him the dollar in that way, what would they have done? Come up with another way, right? Relate that to your own life, and try to make all your efforts, including the reading of this book, with relaxation, love, and joy, because it is given to you to succeed, and for no other reason. That is good news. So give it your best, but give it your joyous best, give it your relaxed best. Because you're offered this help so that you will flourish.

Chapter 25
Microbe Hunters

One of the rooms in my South Bronx apartment was filled with books. It wasn't that I had an inordinately literate family – some people just never get rid of their books. Since our library room was sparsely used, I commandeered it as a place to set up my electric trains. My "O" type model trains were mounted on a 4' x 8' sheet of plywood in the middle of the room. Sometimes I would use the different books to prop up my train tracks, to make a hill, or cause an accident with the lumber loader or the milk cars.

One of the thicker books I used was called *Microbe Hunters,* and it was written by Anton van Leeuwenhoek. He lived around the turn of the 17th century, and was one of the early researchers into micro-pathology, diseases caused by bacteria and viruses. Every once in a while, I would flip through one of my train track supports, and maybe even read a few lines. It interested me a bit, though I never read much at any one time. Basically, his thesis was that everything started from something smaller than it was, and eventually grew into a recognizable entity that could be named. Like a tree for example. Disease was his target example, with bacteria being the microcosm of disease. In other words, if you have pneumonia, you at one time had only a tiny *pneum*, and even before that you had an itsy bitsy *pne*.

He dedicated his life to both research, and trying to convince the scientific community that there was a basis to his premise – all disease begins as a micro-particle, and eventually grows into its recognizable extension. The full–grown thing was just a whole lot of little disease-ettes. Like a flood is a collection of drops of water, and it's the quantity that causes a very different impact from the individual drop. Even at an early age I was curious about this assertion, not that I was interested in its medical applications – kids don't think about diseases much.

This idea that was interesting to me then, still absorbs me now. In fact, it has become part of the practice with which I have involved myself. That is, to study the awakening of consciousness, truth, and enlightenment by trying to reduce it to micro-particles, in both its positive aspect, and what obstructs us from it.

I have found this study to be fascinating, informative, and most of all, useful. It must surely be valuable, were we to discover within us, the seed of the obstacles to the experience of freedom and awakened consciousness – an experience we know is our birthright, but in everyday life is still so shrouded from us. This study that I have made is an investigation of obstacles and mini-particles of these obstacles, and how we contract, and more importantly, how we maintain the diseases of fear, jealousy, arrogance, boredom, and anger. All these diseases shroud us from beauty and truth.

Like Anton van Leeuwenhoek, I have proceeded with the premise that, though it is too painful for us to even acknowledge the existence of these diseases in their full-blown form, much less assault them, perhaps their micro-particles are vulnerable to penetration, or at least to scrutiny.

One of the discoveries from my research has been that we need not permanently lose the innocence, the inner connection, or the hope with which we began this life. And one of the keys to regaining that purity of heart, is to recognize that it got lost in increments.

Now you know another reason why I've written this book. If somebody knows that there really is reason to hope, then that person should be making some noise. So I'm doing that.

Chapter 26
The Right Questions

After having visited Russia, I've become somewhat interested in their history, and am doing some reading on that subject. I have been reading about the idea of knowing the right questions to ask, in terms of Soviet/American history and World War II. Putting energy into answering questions, calls up the relevance of asking the correct ones. This has been reflected historically in some of the events I've been reading about.

At some point toward the end of the war, the leaders of the Soviet Union, Britain, and the U.S. – who were Stalin, Churchill, and Roosevelt, got together at a place called Yalta, and talked about what to do, since the war was close to being over. The Americans had already landed in Europe, and the British and the French were already close to invading Germany, and liberating whatever had to be liberated there. Churchill's understanding was very different than Roosevelt's. Roosevelt saw Stalin as an ally, because Russia had been fighting the Germans, and the U.S. had been fighting the Germans for all those years. The Russians had lost millions of people, so Roosevelt even had an endearing name for his ally – Uncle Joe. Whereas Churchill was perpetually suspicious of Russian expansionism, and didn't want to allow Stalin any foothold in Europe or Asia.

The American Secretary of State was trying to figure out the best way to negotiate with Stalin – what to give him, and what not to give him, and how he was going to continue to be our ally. Churchill, on the other hand, was starting to set up a strategy for his new enemy. The questions he was asking were about how to deal with this enemy Russia, while the U.S. was asking how to deal with this ally Russia.

As it turned out, the American policy-makers were asking the wrong questions, and putting an incredible amount of energy into making the decision of what to relinquish and what not to relinquish. The American government eventually agreed to give Russia all of Eastern Europe, and some islands off Japan. The Americans were still fighting Japan, and wanted the Russians to join in, which they hadn't to this point.

That was totally a mistake because the Russians never did do that. All our strategy, and all our questions, and all the energy that we put into answering those questions were a waste of time, because they were the wrong questions. The questions should have been more aligned with Churchill's questions: *How do we contain this enemy?* not, *How do we appease this ally?*

Without going further into history, I want to liken that to our situation, because I see it very similarly. I see that some of us have been very energetic in researching and answering questions for our own betterment – our physical betterment, our emotional betterment, and our spiritual betterment. We have been energetic in that regard, but from my view, our questions have been wrong. So all the energy that people are putting into answering those questions is as much a waste of time as it was for the American government in WWII – because we are asking the wrong questions. We are asking so many questions about our physical well-being. We are asking so many questions about our environmental well-being. We are asking so many questions about our political, social, and financial well-being.

So many answers, so much information has been gathered about what foods are healthy, what environment is healthy, what is unhealthy, what is moderately healthy, what you should stay away from. We don't recognize that there is an enemy within, and that enemy is not being addressed by your questions, and subsequently it is not being addressed by your answers. Until you address the correct questions, you're not going to be getting any answer that could possibly lead you to inner peace, to spiritual reconnection, or to any of the inner aspirations that people have historically had.

This might be an example of an attempt to ask the right questions. Some years ago I decided I would take a group of people on an expedition. It was the first time I considered doing that with people who I was responsible for. Fifteen of us went on a trip to the Andes Mountains in Peru. We went there for an extended period of time – some of us for three months, others for a month or two. Some care had to be taken in preparation for a trip that involved getting away from civilization to places where dangers might exist, or at least conditions that could be extremely physically challenging.

This wasn't to be a tour of the capital cities. So I decided we would do extensive research in the areas that were necessary to make sure that I could at least, what's known as, *bring 'em back alive*. In order to do this research, we would have to ask and answer some critical questions, and ignore other issues that would work themselves out along the way. Because I hadn't done anything like this before, I wasn't sure of the spiritual advantages of this type of trip. Since then I have learned a lot about the assets and liabilities of such a venture.

We separated our research into different areas – food, health, safety, climate, equipment and whatever else seemed relevant to explore in advance. One of the areas that we explored extensively was health issues – what shots to get, what shots not to get, what places to avoid – because yellow fever and tuberculosis are endemic in some areas of Peru.

It was really important to do this research, not so much to be afraid, or to be paranoid, or to be looking around for disease everywhere, but to ask the right questions in order to become informed about what actually were the dangers. I thought it was a worthwhile undertaking because we were becoming informed, and we were getting to work together to discern what the right questions were.

Think of your life right now. Almost all of your energy goes into answering questions that will not lead you to where you think they're going to lead you. You are not informed about where the dangers are, and if you happen to be somewhat informed, you're not well enough informed.

That's where the concept of self-study comes in. Because the dangers clearly are not coming from without, they are coming from within. You are the enemy. You are also the ally, but you are the enemy. You have to learn to distinguish between the way in which you are your worst enemy, and the way in which you are your best friend. Learning to ask the right questions will help you to unravel this complex labyrinth.

Chapter 27

Cat Hair & Ground Glass

I used to have a constant tickle in my throat. I thought it was something that I was going to have to live with for my whole life. Finally I went to an allergist, because it was getting overly troublesome. I was living in a really damp area, which seemed to aggravate my condition. The doctor asked if I had a cat, and when I told him I did, he said it wasn't necessary for him to examine me.

"So I have a cat. What's that got to do with it?"

"Get rid of the cat, and you'll get rid of the tickle," the medic said confidently.

My confidence in the medical profession is minimal anyway – my step-father having been a doctor. After hearing him on the telephone prescribing the same thing 2,000 times, I kind of lost confidence. He had his favorite diagnoses which he seemed to apply to everyone – like fibromyalgia, these days. So when the allergist said, "You have a cat? Get rid of it." I said, "Yeah, sure, give me the examination anyway." It turned out he was right. I loved the cat, so I didn't get rid of her, but when her allotted time was over, the tickle was over too. It's important that you know about my ex-tickle, and you're about to find out why.

Years ago I was traveling from San Diego to Seattle. At that time, one of the ways I got around was with drive-away cars. If you've ever done a drive-away car, you know that there are agencies that advertise for drivers to drive their clients' cars from place A to place B. It can be an economical way to travel, but of course, at that time gas was cheaper.

On this particular occasion, I went to the drive-away agency, and they didn't have any cars going that far north. So I looked in the paper and found a private ad for somebody who wanted their car driven to Seattle. It was approaching the deadline for when I had to be up north, so I couldn't be too choosy about the car. I had to take the first car that came along, even if it was an oldie. I called the number in the ad, and we agreed on an arrangement and a time to pick up the car.

I don't remember anything about the car owner, but I do remember that when he showed me the car, I was pleased to see that it was a late model. What I wasn't pleased to see, was that there was cat hair all over the back seat of the car. I said to myself, "Oh no, what am I gonna do?" At that point I knew I was allergic to cats, and the car was full of cat hair. He was talking details about the car, and I wasn't listening, because I was talking to myself about what I was going to do. Of course I wasn't telling him this, because I knew I had to take the car.

I came up with the idea that I would roll down the windows, and drive the 1,500 miles with my head out of the window. It was no problem at all near San Diego, because the weather was nice. All the windows were rolled down and I wasn't having any trouble with my tickle. Of course, every once in a while, I looked in the back and saw the hair and thought, "Oh my God," but so far I was okay. You know the way it is when you imagine something is happening, but it isn't happening – at least not yet.

I drove past San Francisco, then up Interstate 5 through the Siskiyou Mountains. Toward the summit it started getting very cold. There's snow up in that area in the winter. I couldn't close the windows, so I pulled over in order to put on all the clothes that I had. I was bundled up and still freezing my ass off. I didn't have gloves, so my hands were freezing too. I was driving, windows down, head out, over the Siskiyou summit into Oregon in the middle of the winter. I was miserable.

Eventually I got the car delivered to Seattle, and that was that. It was one of the most unpleasant rides that I have ever taken. Not only because of the cold, but more because I never stopped debating, "Should I close the windows? I can't close the windows. Should I close the windows? I'm freezing my ass off. What should I do?"

I delivered the car to the address where this guy from San Diego was going to move. I knocked on the door and a woman opened it. As it swung open, I looked in and saw two dogs – and right then I realized. So the first thing I said to her was, "Does this guy have cats?" She said, "No, he has two dogs. These are his dogs. He told me he mentioned it to you – about all the dog hair in the back."

The whole event from beginning to end rushed before me. I realized my misery was unnecessary, because this guy had dogs and not cats, and I wasn't allergic to dogs. In San Diego, instead of listening to his explanation about the dog hair, I was talking to myself about how I would deal with the cat hair. He was probably apologizing to me about the dog hair in the back of his car. Not only did I go through all of that discomfort for not paying attention, but my paranoia was so strong, that the possibility of it being dog hair never even occurred to me. I was so sure that I was dealing with the maximum potential problem.

This story, pitiful but true, exemplifies one obstacle from which we must get free – our self-destructive proclivity for imagining and dreading the worst possible eventuality. In order to get free of such a tendency, each person must know, at every moment, whether there is a possibility of some self-destructive activity going on. Our self-destructive activities may not have the power of the beneficence and the grace of the Creator, but neither does a cloud have that power in relation to the sun, but still they can make things look pretty dark.

A TV movie I saw recently, told a similar story in a far less humorous manner. You might find it less entertaining, but it certainly highlights the need for freedom from this particular obstacle. It was about a woman who was poisoning her husband by feeding him minuscule amounts of very fine ground glass, which was undetectable, but had the effect of slowly killing him. Slowly but surely he was dying, and there was no way that it could be diagnosed.

This guy was eating ground glass mixed up in his goulash, never realizing that he was being poisoned. He was going to physicians, chiropractors, physical therapists, faith healers, getting every possible type of treatment, remedy, and help. Of course it was clear for at least one person, the person who was stirring in the ground glass, that none of this could conceivably do any good. So here was this man saying, "I have a headache today. Maybe I'll try some of these little teeny homeopathic pills." They were his next hope for relief – his next possibility.

Eventually he went down the list of every possible remedy and every possible medical test. Nothing was working, because there was no correlation between any of the medication and the real problem. There could have been a correlation, if that person had a disease that wasn't being regenerated every day with a new dose of ground glass. But as it was, there was no correlation whatsoever. His health was going downhill fast. He was trying all kinds of things. He didn't know what was going on. He was being destroyed, but had no idea what it was that was doing the destroying.

My diagnosis of the human condition is very similar to the eventual posthumous diagnosis of this person. People are imagining that they are performing actions to improve their condition, when in fact they are not aware of the source of the condition that needs improving. This man also had a problem. Unfortunately his ignorance of the source of the problem made what he was doing to alleviate it a waste of time.

After reading the above story, I see that the theme of it, and the cat hair story are somewhat different. It probably would have fit better in the previous chapter, but since both stories are interesting, and there is still a common denominator, I will continue anyway.

The solutions that we're presented with, for the difficulties we experience, don't refer to either the actual problem or the requisite solution. So not only are we not getting the solutions for our problems, but we're presenting the wrong problems. We're getting solutions to problems that aren't really there. What if everything you put forth as the difficulty, everything you put forth as needing to be solved, is not the problem?

It's like adding oil when you run out of gas. You don't have any extra oil so you go to the store. They're out of your brand of oil. They have to order it. After a week you go to the store to pick it up. You forget your wallet and you have to go home. You still don't have the oil. Then you finally get the can, you bring it home and you don't have something to open it with. So you go find a puncher for the can. You're doing all this to put more oil in your car, but you aren't low on oil. You're out of gas. The whole time you're thinking oil, and oil isn't the problem.

What you profess to be missing in your life is not what's missing. The answers you get to the questions you pose, may be answers to the questions you pose. But they're not the answer to the problem – because they're not the problem. What you think is wrong is not what's wrong.

There is a very direct parallel between the situation of the man eating the ground glass and our lives, because every day we are ingesting something, or more accurately, performing actions that are regenerating a disease that we, as contemporary humans, share. So even if you're doing something with your left hand that could alleviate your condition, you are doing something at least as self-destructive with your right hand – something that would put you back to where you first started, because, unbeknownst to you, the problem is regenerating itself, not only day to day, but moment to moment.

That's a very profound diagnosis to propose. It's almost too much to accept. Think of all the things that you do to improve your lot – to help your situation – to make it so that you become a *have,* in the ways that you see yourself as still being a *have-not* – whether it be material, problematic, relationship-oriented, physical, mental, emotional, political, sexual, social – whatever! What if the things that you are doing to improve your life, are not the things that are actually going to improve it?

Whatever improvement-oriented practice you may be presently pursuing, or whatever practice you eventually plan to pursue – whether it's traditional religion, meditation-based, or analytical – some facet of that method must also include discovering what it is that you do to slide two steps backward, after you've been successful at gaining two steps forward. If you don't find out what self-destructive tendencies are causing those backward steps, you can do whatever the priest tells you, or the guru tells you, or the doctor tells you, or your friends tell you, or the book tells you. As beneficial as all their suggestions may be, and however good your intentions, you will not get anywhere. Your progress will be arrested, unless you know intimately, for yourself, what it is that you're doing simultaneously with these potentially helpful endeavors, to obliterate that progress.

I got an email from my daughter who just had a baby some months ago. She sent me a very cute video of the baby crawling. The baby happened to be crawling backwards – everything else was in order, except the baby was crawling backwards. Every once in a while, my daughter came into the picture and kind of tweaked her around, so she would crawl forward, but basically she was looking to crawl backwards. I did recognize something in that video that I think is important to understand.

If this baby were crawling forward, and we were not aware that forward was the appropriate direction to crawl, (because everyone in the world was crawling backwards), we would then correct that baby, by tweaking her from crawling forwards to crawling backwards. That baby would look around and have affirmation of her crawling, by seeing that other humans in her field of vision were also crawling backwards. Not only was she being corrected from crawling forwards to crawling backwards, but she was witnessing that crawling backwards was the appropriate way to ambulate.

I'm using this nonsensical example because from my perspective and experience, the human race is crawling backwards. And you, as part of the human race, even if you're unaware of it, are also crawling backwards. Crawling backwards is a way to move around, but one that creates another reality, because you have to dedicate some of your energy to taking care of your stiff neck. If you're crawling backwards, you can't see where you're going, unless you spend a good deal of energy compensating for the fact that your head and your eyes face forward. You're having to take care of things that otherwise wouldn't have to be considered if you were crawling forward. You are setting up equipment and systems, and arranging your logistics, and paying substantial amounts of money to chiropractors, to make it so that crawling backwards works out.

What if there were some missing components in our understanding of how to be a human being, and this was causing us to live in the opposite way as was naturally granted to us? What if there were some elemental confusion about what's necessary, and what's not necessary to live a fulfilled human life? If that were so, we might actually be moving backwards. If, as we look around, everyone else was doing what we're doing, it makes sense to move backwards – it's what's happening. Moving backwards becomes the natural thing, because we're observing it all around us. But it's not the natural thing. There are missing pieces in our understanding – actual realities that have eluded us. We may have built our lives on a defective premise, on a faulty concept.

All your corrections, all the work on your stiff neck, all the other things that have come about because of your misconception about how life is supposed to be led and experienced, may be misdirected. All the additions that you have made, all the understanding that you have, and the rights and wrongs and concepts that you have, may be faulty – because they are based on a misconception.

It may be, that if you have all the money you need, and all the health you need, and all the chiropractors you need, you can make it acceptable to walk backwards in life. But there is no reality in it. It's self-maintained. It isn't maintained by any creative force beyond human construction. It's like buildings that we build. They need maintenance, because they're created by humans. Anything that *we* create needs maintenance. We are so involved in our maintenance, because *we* have created the reality that we live in.

Chapter 28

Carousel

Sunday is my best day for working out at the gym. If you've ever used a Stairmaster, you would understand how that could be. You probably also would know that the key to endurance on an exercise machine is diversion, not strength. What I mean is, I can ride the Stairmaster for an amount of time directly proportional to the amount of entertainment I can consume – videos, newspapers, magazines, even the Auto Trader.

To go beyond thirty minutes would be hell, if I couldn't take my thoughts away from the eventual fatigue, breathlessness, and sometimes even nausea. Last Sunday I was reading the reason why Sundays are good workout days – the Los Angeles Times. When I got to the Calendar section, the one that has the movies, etc., I saw an advertisement for a Broadway show that reminded me of something I've wanted to write about, but never got around to.

There are new Broadway shows produced each year, but the popular shows (I guess you could call them classics) are regenerated frequently, not only in New York, but all around the country. For some reason people like to see them over and over again. Often these regurgitated classics are musicals, and the one to which this Times advertisement referred was called *Carousel*. If we were in the same room right now, I might be able to sing a few lines from *It Was A Real Nice Clambake,* or *My Boy Bill,* or *When You Walk Through a Storm* (probably the best known tune from that show), but since we're not, I'll do the next best thing. I'll tell you why I can remember the names and words to songs I haven't heard since my childhood, even though that kind of music is certainly not what I listen to now. You see, *Carousel* was the first Broadway show I ever saw, and I remember something from that Saturday matinee even more clearly than I remember the lyrics.

Living in New York and going to Broadway shows are not synonymous occurrences. Over the span of my childhood I attended many, solely because of the influence of my mother. She was, in those days, an enthusiastic organizer of activities for kids. So much so, that when I was six or seven years old, she formed a kids' club that she named the Jolly Midgets – mostly comprised of my older sister's friends. It was humiliating, but that was our name. I was the midgetest Jolly Midget of them all, because I was two years younger than everybody else. We even had jackets that said Jolly Midgets on the back. Mom was very much into enculturating us by taking us from the Bronx, where we lived, to museums and shows in Manhattan. The common denominator of all those excursions, were the bag lunches of soggy tuna sandwiches – I remember those too.

Carousel was not only my first Broadway show, but the theater in which it played was my first live theater, so all of it was a fascination for me. Broadway theaters have steep balconies, because they try to fit the greatest number of people in the smallest area, and that's where we sat. The height above the stage was a thrill in itself. I was fascinated by the scene. Finally, the thirty piece orchestra started to play, and as I looked down at the huge red velvet curtains, somebody popped out of the seam in the middle and said, "I have an announcement." The announcement was that the man who usually played Billy Bigelow (the star) was sick, and the part would instead be played by somebody else, called an understudy – and then something about refunds.

This announcement meant nothing to me of course, but not so for the other theater-goers. I knew this because a spontaneous groan emerged from the theater, which caused me to immediately look to my mother in the possibility that we were about to have a fire drill.

She was sitting a few seats away, so I didn't get an immediate explanation, and the other kids didn't know any more about what was going on than I. We just sat there and looked at each other, as a number of people started to get up and walk out of the theater. I didn't know what was going on – I didn't even have any idea what live theater was going to look like. All I knew, was what was in front of me – a huge red velvet curtain and a live orchestra, so I knew it wasn't a movie. And I knew something else – the last thing in the world I wanted to do was leave.

My mother got us together at half time, or intermission, which is what they call it at Broadway shows. She explained that this man, the star, who a lot of people came to see, wasn't going to be there. Some people were disappointed enough that they wanted to leave and get their money back, and they were entitled to do that. Other people, like us, didn't care, so they stayed.

Even though it wasn't crystallized in my thoughts, I understood, even at that young age, that there was a lesson to be learned from that outing. That lesson might best be described as: Just because everyone is in the same place, doesn't mean that they have the same reason for being there. Additional observations that I have made over the years, both in my own behavior, and that of others, has only compounded my assurance in this behavioral theory.

We assume that all the students in a college classroom, or all the patients in a hospital emergency room, or all the employees in a business office, are there for the same reason. We assume that unanimity of purpose goes along with the uniqueness of a circumstance. But what began as a fledgling cognition at *Carousel,* has become a full-blown conviction. There are many reasons why one would be at a Broadway show, and similarly, and more relevant at this moment, there are many reasons why a person would be reading this book.

There was a time when you could assume that anyone watching a football game was a fan. With the advent of the Dallas Cowboys cheerleaders that all changed. Soon, all professional sports teams had cheerleaders, and the days of the purest fan were over. I wrote this during the current year's NBA basketball playoffs. If you're not a fan, that's the Super Bowl of professional basketball.

Last night I went on the computer to the site that had the starting times and TV station for anybody who wanted to watch the game. There was a link to a YouTube right next to the schedule that showed the Golden State Warriors' cheerleaders. I wasn't particularly interested in watching the cheerleaders, and the game was already on, so I didn't have time to click on it, even if I was. Seeing the link brought up a few thoughts about this idea of cheerleading, and not only in relation to sports where it's most prolific, but in relation to our lives as well.

I was picturing a locker room where the coach gets his team together and says some inspiring words like, "You can do it, we're great, give 'em hell," and then they all do what's called *take a knee* and say a prayer. This pre-game ritual usually goes on for a while, but it doesn't go on and on and on and on. It eventually ends, because all the players are clear that they are being pumped up, inspired, and motivated to accomplish something.

The end product is not the encouragement. The end product is getting out there and doing your best and winning. If you went to a basketball game, and were watching cheerleaders get out on the floor and do their thing before the game, sooner or later you would want them to get off the floor, and let the athletes play. Even the cheerleaders themselves recognize that at some point they want the game to start. As obvious as this might be, there is a recent phenomenon where cheerleading has actually become an end in itself.

Although I am a sports fan, I am not now writing about that subject. The parallel I see relates to cheerleading in the area of inspiration. It's possible that the concept of inspiration has been distorted to the point that it has become an end in itself. In actuality, one has to be inspired *to do* something, not just be inspired. Inspiration requires a "to." In these times, people are attracted to lectures, movies, and books that are inspiring; but no action is taken from that stimulus, so no change ever really happens. People make an end product out of a continuing succession of inspiring activities, but never get out onto the field and fight, fight, fight.

Chapter 29
Let's Pretend

In the late '70s I lived in Washington, D.C. One of my friends worked for the government, and from time to time would get passes to sit in the gallery, and watch a session of Congress. I went with him one time, and we watched the Senate discuss the Iran hostage crisis. Before the Senators entered the hall, the observers seated in the balcony got a lecture about behavior and protocol.

During the session, there was a heated back and forth between a couple of senators, and some guy near us in the balcony shouted down his opinion on the subject. The guy behind the desk in front banged his gavel and said, "Order, order," and it was quiet again. A couple of minutes later another guy in the balcony shouted something out.

The Sergeant at Arms, who has the job of maintaining order, got up and directed his words to the balcony. "You have no status is these proceedings. You are a guest observer, not a participant. If you want to become a participant, you would have to get 15,000 people to sign a petition. Then you would have to raise a minimum of three million dollars. Then you would have to win a primary election. Then you would have to win a general election. Until you accomplish all those things, you are a guest and an observer. You may be in the building in which the Senate convenes, but you are not in the Senate. You are welcome to get the feeling of what it is like, as long as you're not disruptive."

This extraordinary address by the Sergeant at Arms reminded me of a friend who dropped out of high school. I met him a few years later, and asked what he'd been doing. He told me he was living in Ann Arbor, Michigan. He said he was trying out for the University of Michigan football team. I was surprised, because I knew U. of M. was a tough school to get into, and he had dropped out of high school. He explained to me that he didn't actually go to U. of M., he just showed up at practice and went through the drills. But when they picked the squad he was really disappointed because his name wasn't called.

I asked him how he thought his name could get called if he snuck into practice. I said, "Did you think you were really trying out for the team?" He told me he didn't, but said with all sincerity, "I really got to feel what it was like."

I asked him if he were going to go back to school and do it for real, and he said the following; "Are you nuts? I'm thinking of going to Durham next year and trying out at Duke."

Every accomplishment requires preliminary steps. You can get the feeling of holiness from sitting in a church, or chanting, or whirling, or praying, or trying to meditate, or doing yoga. But that feeling does not reflect your state of being. It reflects a possibility of what *could* be your state of being. And that possibility will only be realized if you are willing and able to take the steps required to make you a participant, not an observer.

A compassionate person, an elevated perspective, a connection with one's Creator – a spiritual life is a very fine vibration. If a person isn't prepared to work to remove the coarseness of their life as it is now, they will never be a participant. Those experiences that give you the feeling of what it would be like to be a participant are precious. But they only point to a possibility. If you make a life of collecting those experiences, you will always be a guest observer. So the question is: Are you looking for another way to get the feeling of what it's like, or are you looking for a way to get it for real?

Chapter 30

Receive, Interpret, Transmit

One way of categorizing human beings, is as entities that serve three functions: to receive, to interpret, and to transmit. What we are receiving, interpreting, and transmitting are vibrations similar in the way that a TV receives, interprets, and transmits the signals that come into it. You will find no picture if you intercept the signal or cut the wire before it reaches a TV. You're not going to see *60 Minutes*, you're going to get a vibration, an impulse, a signal. The TV receives, interprets, and transmits. Its interpretation is a picture and a sound.

We are similar organisms. We receive, interpret, and transmit as well. We receive vibrations, we interpret vibrations, and we transmit vibrations. The vibrations are objective – they are what they are – but our interpretation is extremely subjective – it is what we make it. That's where our life experience comes in. Our life experience is our translation – our interpretation of the vibrations that we receive. Our life experience is totally subjective, and depends on the way we interpret it. We are all receiving many of the same vibrations, and many similar ones as well, but it is in our interpretation that the different experiences of life occur.

When the phone rings, everyone hears the same sound, receives the same vibration, but one person worries, and another is elated – same reception, different interpretation. You're sunning yourself on the beach, and you hear a jet ski out in the water. You react negatively, because your peace and quiet is being disturbed, but the person next to you is excited, because they want to try a jet ski and didn't know they were available on that beach. Both of you heard and saw the same thing, the same auditory and visual vibrations, but your experiences (interpretations) were very different – reception and interpretation. Our interpretation of the vibrations we receive is our experience of life.

You've been reading this (receiving this vibration) for a couple of minutes. One reader is thinking, "Wow, this is blowing my mind. This is incredible!" Somebody else receiving the identical vibration is thinking, "I hope he gets to something interesting, because I've heard all this before." Another reader is also receiving the identical vibration and thinking, "This is too heady, I can't follow it. I just can't follow it. Why doesn't he ever talk about love?" One vibration received by three people results in three different interpretations – three different experiences of the moment. Your reception is vibrational, your interpretation is the subjective experience of your life.

The closer you are to the source of the signal (the origin of the vibration), the clearer your interpretation is likely to be. The further you are from the source of the signal (the vibration), the more distorted your interpretation is likely to be. That's the way it is with the internet, the TV, the radio, the telephone, and that's the way it is with us. Vibrations become less and less fine as they travel away from their source. If your picture is breaking-up, you have to get closer to the sender.

In order to achieve less distortion when interpreting the vibrations we receive, we have to receive them closer to the sender, where the vibration is still relatively fine. Not long ago I put up a satellite dish. Before that, our TV picture was distorted, but now it's clear. Everybody viewing those shows, the news, a sporting event, will think, "Oh, this is clearer. Now I don't have to figure out if that's a football, or is that the guy's head." The vagueness will be gone. The beauty will be more evident. It's the same with us. Vibrations are being sent out, they are everywhere.

We need to learn to receive those vibrations a little closer to the source, just a little closer. We don't have to take a trip to the sun to get tan. We just have to go to Puerto Rico, or maybe even go outside today, but we do have to come out of the house. To get a little closer to the fineness of that vibration, we don't have to go that far, but we do have to remove a few roofs, a few walls, a few obstacles. If we can get a clearer signal, and make a more accurate interpretation, our whole experience of life will change. We will become an instrument of something beautiful. We will then transmit a clearer signal that other people can receive. Our experience will be different, a little closer, a little finer, a little closer to the source, not so distorted, a different life experience. It will be a relief for all of us, but mostly it will be a relief for you.

If our receptions are relegated to the coarse end of the vibration, our interpretations will probably follow suit. Life will appear uninspiring and repetitious. Things like personal possessions will become overly important. Most people have some perspective about the actual importance of personal possessions, but there are people who don't. There are people who have a miserable day, or days, when their car gets dinged. The metal is bent, so their day is bent. There are people who are receiving vibrations that are extremely distorted, and they cannot interpret their importance in any other way, but to consider material objects as so real to them that they are willing to sacrifice a day's experience of life in lament of that dinged door.

Maybe a politician or a financier is caught embezzling, or doing something that many other people have thought about, but not had the courage to do. That person is so humiliated, so embarrassed about how people see them, that they would consider taking their own lives over their loss of reputation. We become embarrassed, withdrawn, apprehensive, nervous, because we don't appear to other people like we want to appear, or aren't thought of as we want to be thought of. Our self-image is real to us. Other people's opinions are so real to us, that we sacrifice the days of our lives to sustain those self-images. That's very far down into the coarse vibrations – the ones that only a truly conscious person can interpret positively.

No one has to have that be their experience of life. But interpretations other than negative ones become very difficult when the vibrations received are no longer fine – the picture is too blurry. The air is cleaner even a little higher up. But you've got to be able to get up there – either that, or learn to give finer interpretations to coarse vibrations. That is what a conscious person can do. If we haven't yet reached that stage, and until we do, we can still put in a satellite dish further up the line, and pick up a purer signal, so that the snow on the TV doesn't cause us to mistake someone's head for a football.

You don't have to pick it up that low; you can get closer to what is. Your life experience depends on it. That a person would interpret their life experience as dependent on a particular resolution of their problems, plans, and relationships, is a very coarse interpretation. It could only be made by a person who has yet to explore the idea of receive, interpret, and transmit.

Annoyance, impatience, self-pity, and embarrassment are all interpretations caused by an unconscious person viewing a coarse vibration. They are distorted interpretations – they are not what is really happening. When a person is no longer confused, they can receive even a coarse vibration and interpret it accurately. But until then, the best chance a person has to achieve an accurate interpretation, is to move closer to the source of the vibration.

The key to receiving a finer vibration is learning to see things as they are, not as we would wish or hope them to be. Things *as they are*, are closer to fine than coarse. Distortion is not part of a fine vibration.

It is important to understand, that learning to receive vibrations closer to their source by seeing things more clearly as they are, is a necessary, but still interim step on the way to learning to interpret all vibrations objectively. There are no negative vibrations – only negative interpretations.

Transmission is part of our function as well. If your interpretations are distorted, then your transmissions will be also. If you wish to be an instrument of peace, you will have to transmit finer vibrations, so that they in turn, can be more easily interpreted accurately by others.

Chapter 31
Rick and Tony

From my first moments of glimpsing possibilities of which I was previously unaware, I became fanatically interested in exploring the subject of consciousness, and still am. In those early years, my lifestyle included going to informal gatherings at people's houses where the central focus, really the only focus, was smoking marijuana and listening to music, with a few breaks for trippy conversation.

I might have known some of the people there, or I might not have – it didn't matter – we were all getting high together. My closest friends were equally enthusiastic about the possibility of expanding consciousness, and we often attended these impromptu get-togethers as a group. During the breaks between the music, we might have had a conversation amongst ourselves about honesty, or awareness, or being real. Sometimes other people from the party would participate or just listen in, and sometimes not.

There was no proselytizing going on. There were no robes involved. We were just a bunch of people getting high together. Eventually some of those close friends moved to California, and shortly after I did also. I found a cabin in the redwoods close to the coast in a place called Pescadero. The redwoods were so dense that it never got very light, so you couldn't tell if it was morning or night. It also rained a lot in the winter, and the only wildlife was big yellow things called banana slugs. I lived there for a year, spending most of my time sitting in front of the fire writing, listening to music, or trying to figure out what my next step was. I really liked the solitude.

Nobody lived in those woods except for a couple of people who had cabins, and we all kept pretty much to ourselves. So it was unusual one afternoon to hear a knock on my door. I got up and looked through the glass and didn't recognize either of the people there. I opened the door and said, "Hi." They asked, "Justin?" And I said, "Yeah?" They said a few words about where they had come from, and I asked them to come on in. There was only one person in the general area that knew where I was, and he lived over the hill in Redwood City, so I assumed that's how they found me.

The three of us sat down in front of the fire, and I brought them some tea. They said they were from the East Coast and had met me there. I told them I didn't remember them, but it was nice to have visitors. I tried to remember meeting them, but had no recollection whatsoever of either of them. Eventually the older guy, Rick, told me that they were at a party about a year before, and heard me talking about some fascinating stuff. Rick was sitting on the stairs behind me and listening to what I had to say. He told me that he never forgot that conversation, and it changed the direction of his life. They rode their motorcycles across the country to find me.

I wasn't a teacher at that time in Pescadero, but when I started my first group in Oregon later that year, Rick and Tony were in it. I've known both of those guys for years and years. I probably wouldn't have crossed paths with them, had I not represented what meant something precious to me at that party. When they overheard me, I was speaking my truth – talking about what was real to me – without fear of embarrassment or anything else. I'm still doing that. How can I stop? Their lives were changed.

Chapter 32

Una Manta

I had a teacher for many years who lived on the border of Peru and Bolivia, near Lake Titicaca. I made numerous trips down there starting when I was actually quite young. He had been a friend of my family, and I originally met him in New York. I eventually went down to live with him for a summer, and visited him sporadically for periods of three and six months, and almost a year one time. Everybody called him Raya, because he was a weaver who wove rugs with knots called raya knots. Not only did he weave for himself, he also wove for the town cooperative, where he was the business manager. Raya had a married sister with a son named Oscar who stayed with Raya sometimes. I met him several times on trips down there, and stayed in his room when he wasn't there.

The first time I had a discussion with Oscar was when I really started to think seriously about things. I was 18 or 19 years old, and was spending the summer with Raya in Peru. After that summer, I had numerous opportunities to talk with Oscar. He was into some kind of martial arts, and was always trying to get me to spar with him. I remember that. At that time I was a bit of a boxer, so we tumbled around a little. It never lasted very long, because he was much older and bigger than I.

I remember him as having an exploratory mind, and being very bright and interested in things. He had a philosophy that I had not been exposed to before that time. He was attracted to miraculous happenings and phenomenal ideas. I liked listening to him because he was smart and well-spoken, but I never connected with the importance he put on the phenomena that he was so into. Oscar went on to become a well-known spiritual teacher, and the founder of an international institute. The first time I asked Raya about Oscar, he explained his own philosophy to me, and how it differed from Oscar's, and I want to try to convey that to you.

Raya's explanation of his own philosophy went like this: The school that has been presented to us is called our life. It need not be formed or established. The learning circumstances that have been presented to us in incredible variety, need not be artificially created. The circumstances that we need, are the circumstances that we're given. Any attempt to *create* a world in which to learn is a misdirection. No one could possibly create a world where learning can happen better than the one that's been created. *Our* job is to not avoid what is in front of us.

I don't remember how that sat with me at first, but obviously something rang true about it. Because at that time, what was really interesting to me was exploring what was, not what might be, and Oscar's focus was the opposite. Raya was very supportive of Oscar. I never heard him say anything negative about him, but this one point was always something that he would bring up about Oscar: Oscar was trying to create a world for spiritual learning, not recognizing that the world that we have has all the components that we need for that learning. Our efforts only have to be supervised by someone who knows how to make use of it.

I have not come to the end of all the possibilities of learning from the world that we have been given, though I have covered many of its bases. I have explored the world of business, the world of power tools, the world of supermarkets, the world of children, parents, cooking, driving, international travel, and building houses. Those worlds are the metaphor for everything that we need to learn. That is the experience of this enlightened human. It's no longer a philosophy that was taught to me, it is my philosophy.

If you pay attention to what is, to what you are in the midst of, whether it be the next bite of your dinner, or an episode in your life, you will have the information, experience, and impressions needed to take the next step. This is a difficult time to present that philosophy. Everything we do appears so mundane to us, that it's impossible for us to see how focusing on the ordinary could possibly yield an extraordinary experience. We expect that only extraordinary circumstances will yield an extraordinary experience.

When I was staying with Raya, I had chores and things he had me take care of. They were the kind of ordinary things that could lead to extraordinary experiences if a person knew how to view them, and was guided by a master of that art.

Raya was the business manager of his area's weaving co-op, so he negotiated to buy wool and sell rugs all over the Andean Altiplano. Sometimes the co-op would get a contract job to weave rugs for an artesan company in Peru's capital, Lima, where they would then be sold all over the world. If Raya had an unusually big job, he would buy wool in large quantities, and have it brought by train or truck to a nearby town called Juliaca, in order to be picked up.

I was there on a visit sometime in my twenties. I already understood some of what Raya was trying to help me to learn, and had developed a considerable amount of respect for his capacity as a teacher. Raya negotiated to buy a large quantity of llama, alpaca, and merino wool for a contract job, which had to be picked up in Juliaca near the railway station. Raya had a way of having twice as many people do something as was needed, because in his opinion, confusion was one of the best potential learning tools we have going for us.

This time he told six of us to go in and pick up the wool. Six people would be doing a job that two people could do, because at the railway station, porters would load for almost nothing. We didn't need so many people, but we all went into town with two wagons that were pulled by mules – two of us in my cart and four in the other cart.

I rode with Fiona, a French woman. I was about twenty-four and she was in her forties and big. I remember that about Fiona – she was large. She was handling the reins, and I was sitting next to her. I don't remember the content of our conversation during that ride, but I do remember how pedantic she was. She was authoritative about anything we talked about. When she said something, that was the way it was. Whatever stories she told were factual, and that was that. At one point she asked me if I knew where hookahs (water-pipes) came from, and I told her that I guessed they came from Turkey. Of course she told me I was wrong. She said they come from further away in Central Asia, and that's how the subject of hookahs came about.

According to Fiona, the actual birth of the hookah, not only was in a small village in Central Asia, but the first one was developed by a woman. Fiona explained in her authoritative manner, that the women of the village used clay pots for baking, and storing food, and hauling water, and this woman introduced a way of smoking that utilized these clay pots. Her way was less abrasive and forced more air into one's lungs, so they would be getting a better mix of air and smoke. She got a clay pot with liquid in it, closed off the top and stuck a pipe out of it, lit it up, and passed it around for others to try. What she didn't realize was that it was somebody's chamber pot – a pot that people pee in so they don't have to go outside at night. So the people smoked from this first hookah, and it blew everyone's mind how mild the smoke was, not knowing that the liquid in the bottom wasn't just water, but a blend.

When they discovered what the liquid was, they found a more appropriate one, and that was the birth of the water pipe according to Fiona. We both had a good laugh, and I savored the moment, thinking that listening to her tell that story would probably be the only pleasant interaction I would ever have with her.

The one thing I neglected to mention, was that Raya put me in charge of the pickup operation. He usually put someone in charge, and as I said, always had two or more times the people needed to do the job, whatever it was. Raya made it clear to everyone involved that I was in charge, and when we went into town, it wasn't only the pickup that I was in charge of – I was responsible for everything that happened, including all the interactions of the group. If we had lunch, I was even responsible for how that went.

We picked up the wool first, and that went smoothly. Then we all went to sit in a place to have some tea or coffee. There were eight of us sitting around a rectangular table – the six of us including Fiona and me, plus the two guys that brought the wool on the train who I invited to join us. While the six of us were drinking either tea or coffee, and the two guys were drinking chicha, a Peruvian beer drink, two Australian hippies sitting nearby came over and asked if we knew of some particular place.

It happened that there was a quasi-spiritual school in the area that had an international reputation, and sometimes hippies from Europe or America would come down and try to find it. So, seeing other Westerners, which you don't see very often in Juliaca, they came over and asked if we knew where the school was.

I was in charge, so I asked them to sit down and join us. We sat there for a while, and they asked some questions, and we gave some answers. It was not comfortable for me to be the head in that situation, as I was the youngest one, but I was supposed to be the head, so I did most of the answering of their question.

After a while they went their way, and we got on the cart and went back to deliver the wool to the storage shed. A few of us went over to Raya and told him that we were back. He asked how it went. Fiona gave Raya a detailed account of what happened, as I held my breath, waiting for her to drop some bomb or other – but she didn't. In fact, she raved about what a great job I did, and how much she liked working with me, and how really together I was in talking to the two Australians . . . go figure. Raya listened to her report and smiled his special smile – that in itself was an extraordinary experience for me.

Weaving is not only done for commerce in this area, it is a popular activity on the Andean Altiplano. It is often done on a back-strap loom. They tie one end to a tree, and the other end goes around them, and they stretch it by leaning back as they weave. The women can often be seen using these looms to weave a cloth about two feet by four feet, which they call *una manta*. These alpaca cloths come exclusively from the area around 12,000-foot-high Lake Titicaca, the highest large lake in the world.

When I wasn't occupied with assignments from Raya, or hanging out with him, I hiked around the mountains and sometimes took a reed boat out on the lake. The last time I was there, I intended to bring back some indigenous articles to make Raya feel more at home, in case he ever came to visit me in the U.S. So I went on what you might call a shopping trip. Not to a mall, but to some of the remote local villages.

I had seen beautiful cloths like these before, but I had not known there was a story behind them. When I went into the first small village on my route, I asked a lady who was sitting and weaving in front of her house if she had any cloths that she wanted to trade or sell. Speaking very understandable Spanish (she was one of the few Aymara Indians in her village that spoke Spanish – of course nobody there speaks English), she told me they only made two of these particular cloths during one's lifetime – one for their babies to be born in, and one to be buried in. That was it.

I said, "Well, if they're that special, I certainly wouldn't want to . . ."

"Oh, no, no, no!" she said, "It's fine." She took me into a room where she had a stack of them made by various members of her family. She said, "You can buy as many of these as you want, because they are the ones that our babies were born in – we don't need them anymore. But," she added, "the ones over there – you can't have those, because they are the ones we will be buried in."

It struck me that there was something profound going on there, so we talked about this custom for a while. I asked, "How about all the time in the middle – between birth and death – do you have special cloths for that time?"

She answered casually, "Oh, it doesn't matter." That's exactly what she said, "No importante."

I was walking to a few more villages on this particular trail, and was curious to find if I would discover similar customs in the next village. Basically, every village that I went to had their own special patterns and colors, but the story was always the same: "Yes, you can buy as many of those 'birth mantas' as you want. Once or twice a year even the people from the shops in the city come up, and we sell to them. But no, you can't have the ones in that pile, because people get buried in those."

"And what about the time in between?" I asked each time.

"Oh, it's incidental. Nothing special is needed for that time."

So let's think about this in a way other than the way we've learned to think about it. The time before we're born is immense, and the time after we're gone is immeasurable, and the time that we're here is minuscule. The weaver's perspective of the situation was – when you arrive it's special, and when you leave it's special, but in the incidental time in between: "No, we certainly wouldn't make one of those beautiful garments for such a brief excursion."

I bought several of those mantas and kept one for myself, which I made into a vest. If you were to see it, you would notice that the workmanship is rough-hewn, but in putting it on, I have the feeling of how relatively incidental is our time of living. Sometimes I remember that it was a manta for somebody's birth. Someone who may very well be gone now. Now they're residing in another manta and going on to the infinity that follows.

We're probably the first culture to change that model of relative importance. According to us, before birth has no importance, and after death has no importance, but THIS – this is big time. The time before our existence has become subject to fancifulness, imagination, and stories of reincarnation and spirits, as has the time after our existence – filled with wishful thinking and imagination. Our lives, covering only the briefest of duration, being the only time that we take totally seriously.

I was reading an astronomy book recently and came upon this number; 87,000,000,000. No, let's not call it 87 billion, because we can't really feel a billion. The word billion rolls off the tongue a little too easily for something that's a thousand times bigger than a million. Let's call it 87 thousand million. We can feel that a little better. One thousand million trucks or dishes or gallons of apple juice – start with a thousand million, and it's 87 times that.

That's a very big quantity of anything. It also happens to be the approximate number of stars in our galaxy. That's right – there are 87 thousand million potential sun-systems in our galaxy. Of course most of them don't have planets around them, so they're not actually systems – some of them do, but most of them don't.

Like it or not, neither we nor any human being will ever leave our solar system. That feat will never be within the capacity of a human being. (If the preceding statement riles you, these words are a must read for you.) There are 87 thousand million suns in our galaxy. So there are 86 thousand million and a whole bunch of 9's suns that we'll never know very much about. That's in one galaxy, our galaxy – the Milky Way. And there are a hundred thousand million other galaxies. One hundred thousand million other galaxies, and each one of those contains thousands of millions of stars.

You probably know of the existence of mantras (not mantas, mantras) – words, whether they be Latin or Hindi or Sanskrit, that people are taught to repeat over and over again to achieve some alteration in consciousness – like "Om Mani Padme Hum" or "Jesus Christ have mercy on me." I was thinking of inventing an English language mantra, since we really don't know what those foreign words mean except in translation.

See what you think of this one: "Our galaxy has 87 thousand million suns. Our galaxy has 87 thousand million suns." Do you think that has a spiritual vibration to it? Or would it better if we said it in Sanskrit? If we weren't ready yet to do real meditation, and had to sit and repeat a mantra, could we imagine the effect of a mantra like that? If we allowed those words to really get to us, think what effect they could have on our self-important attitude.

No meaningful answer is going to come to any of our deeper questions, until we feel our appropriate place in a creation in which there are 87 thousand million suns in a hundred thousand million galaxies. Then the questions we ask will weigh about a millionth of a featherweight, and the answers will be just as light. The questions that we're asking now, and the answers that we're giving to those questions, all weigh more than we weigh. Our self-importance distorts our view.

We never learned to have an accurate perspective of our relative importance, so we don't know much about it. We haven't tripped over it. If we did trip over it, we tripped over it on the way somewhere, and didn't even notice it was there. It was there, then it was gone. Sometimes we flash back on moments when we were clear about what it is to be a human being – maybe a woman giving birth to a child. In that moment she had a feeling of being one billionth part of things. Power was moving her. But it's not now. It's not in this moment. This moment we feel like we're bigger than we really are.

Even our everyday problems are compounded by this self-importance. Without a self-important "me," there is no huge "my problem." Certainly we have practical matters to deal with, and sometimes they can become troublesome, but our obsession with the importance of our problems only multiplies their negative effect.

We're living as prisoners of a distorted sense of our own importance, and we've got to get free of it. What's needed to get free is an inner perspective of being an infinitesimal part of a creation that contains 87 thousand million suns. Then we'll only need to absorb our portion of breath – not all the breath. That fraction that we absorb, that one hundred thousand millionth of one 87 thousand millionth of the breath that's delivered, times all the beings that have breath, that is what we can call our life. That one fraction of all that breath gives us our life, and is what *is* our life. To experience that reality is an answer to freedom from our self-importance.

Learning a critical lesson about the distortion of self-importance while buying cloth on a walk in the hills is what Raya was talking about, and I'm writing about now. We don't have to construct a world in which to learn – whether it be an ashram, a monastery, or a cloister. The world that we have has all the components that we need for that learning. Our efforts only have to be supervised by someone who knows how to make use of it.

Chapter 33

The Shinto Temple

Having long-term contacts in foreign places can be critical when a large number of people want to spend a few months doing service work. My friends and I have worked alongside Daughters of Charity nuns on numerous occasions, so when one of those nuns asked us to come to Cambodia and build an addition onto one of their clinics, we knew it was time to take another service trip.

After spending that incredibly rich time in Cambodia, several of us flew home by way of Japan. I like to break up long flights whenever possible. Having some regular sleep keeps the effects of jetlag to a minimum. We spent about thirty-six hours outside of Tokyo in Narita, a small town with the same name as the international airport, but esthetically very removed from it.

The next morning we went to visit a local Shinto temple which was set in the middle of 20-30 acres of very exotic and beautifully manicured grounds. Everywhere I've been in Japan, the land and buildings have consistently been extremely well cared for and spotlessly clean.

While we were walking around, I saw that there was a ceremony just about to be initiated in the main temple. I decided to sit in there for a while. I became aware of the upcoming ceremony because not far away from where I was standing, the principles of the ceremony, twelve men in exotic cloaks, formed a solemn procession that led into the temple. Not only were they wearing ornately colored silk robes, but wooden double horizontal platform shoes that seemed impossible to walk in. If you have ever seen a woman with five inch heels walking on a cobblestone street and wondered how in the world she could do that – this looked even harder.

Inside the temple there were probably a couple of hundred people sitting and chanting in the familiar guttural sound of the Buddhist chant, and as I was learning, the Shinto chant as well. There is a certain sound that they were going for – an imitation of their history I assume.

The ceremony lasted about fifteen minutes and consisted of that chanting, plus some praying and bowing, after which everyone except the twelve men in wooden platform shoes filed out silently. I was left sitting there alone, as those twelve men – monks I guess – were, you might say, cleaning up after the ceremony. There appeared no necessity to leave, so I got to watch that part of the process, and that's the part I want to write about.

It may reveal something about my perspective and what, perhaps, was their perspective. There was an obvious ritual that they went through, composed first of the ceremony, and a second that I was observing, that took place in the cleanup phase after the ceremony.

Toward the back of the room there were six sizable candles set in candelabras. They were as high as the monk whose job it was to snuff out their flame. He walked from candle to candle with a bell-shaped snuffer which was affixed to the end of an ornate metal wand. He took probably thirty minutes doing this job of extinguishing the flame of six candles.

I sat there for the whole time, and in my task of watching, had as much interest as he seemed to have in his task of snuffing. He went over to each candle, paused in front of it as if it were an altar, and carefully and gracefully raised his wand and snuffed it out. As if that wasn't ceremonial enough, he proceeded to meticulously go around the candle with another tool to clean the excess wax, after which he straightened the wick and snipped off the top. Then he walked slowly to the next candle and the next – each candle of the six taking about five minutes.

This was the ritual that he performed. This was his assigned job to be carried out after the ceremony. I sat there fascinated, watching such impeccability in addressing this simple task. But this attitude was not only manifested by the candle monk. One of the other monks was dusting off the fallen incense ash from one of the flat wooden shiny surfaces. As he spent a similar five minutes dusting each area where there was incense ash, the other monks were also occupied with their heavily ritualized post-ceremony chores. I got to observe their very concentrated and you might even say *state of presence* bearing with what they were doing, even though it was something they had done many, many times before.

The reason, other than the obvious one of the uniqueness of the scene, that this phenomenon interests me is because the recognition of the importance of ritual is something with which I have had some experience. Exploring the nature of ritual has led me to believe that in most, if not all cases, the result of ritual is that it supplants or takes the place of essential understanding. The more concentrated the ritual, the more perfection there is in its carrying out, the less understanding there is of the original reason for the practice that existed before it became a ritual. The process of the ritual becomes the reality, and the reason that one is doing it and where it all comes from disappears.

Certainly ritualistic imitation can be beautiful, even captivating to watch, but as anyone who has explored this phenomenon recognizes, the more that you perfect and learn the gestures exactly as they are supposed to be, the less you remember, not only whatever you might have known about its purpose, but why you got into it in the first place. Of course you do become an adept practitioner, and this can be a source of both status, and a feeling of belonging to a tradition.

In my view, participation in ritual is a subtle but definite nemesis. This nemesis connects us with the past in a destructive way, not in the way regard for the past should, and could be experienced and appreciated. Ritual is an imitation of something that happened last time, and by doing it this time, you are not creating your reality in the moment, but are trying to live a past reality.

Chapter 34
Declaration of Dependence

I was traveling in Europe and crossed paths with some guys who wanted to drive to India in their Land Rover. I had no direction home at the time, so when they asked me if I wanted to go along, I said sure. As I remember, it was grueling and not much fun, but we did eventually get to Pakistan when I had enough of them. They rated how well the trip was going, by how many miles they made in a day.

My guidebook said that there were some beautiful beaches in southern Pakistan around Karachi, and after bouncing around for two weeks I was about ready for some of that. I convinced them to head south to Karachi and the Arabian Sea, where these beaches were supposed to be – and eventually we found Clifton Beach.

Whatever the words are when a beautiful beach is being described, those were the words in the guidebook – untouched beach, white sand, azure water, all that stuff. The first thing we saw after we parked and walked down to the water, was a trench down the middle of the beach from the local village into the ocean – and you know what that trench was used for. That's the sewage system, and this beach had one going right down the middle. Not one to be discouraged, I figured we would only have to walk up the beach for a while to find the white sand and azure water. I don't remember if my traveling companions went with me or not, but I walked maybe a quarter of a mile and voilà – there was another trench down the beach from a different community, with the appropriate grey matter and blue garbage bags floating in it. I wasn't prepared to give up yet, so I walked down to the other end of the beach, and the same thing happened again.

Eventually I had to reassess the situation. I had to acknowledge that the premise I was following was leading nowhere. It was hard to do, since I had so looked forward to some relief from the unpleasant ride. The only other choice was to pretend it wasn't really sewage, that it was actually something else, and swim at this beach – and that was no choice at all.

The reason I am mentioning this, is because all of us, mostly through what we have heard or read, have adopted fanciful concepts, and have developed hopes based on those concepts. Some of those concepts might be, that wealth leads to happiness, or that peace comes as a result of controlling circumstances, or that being independent and not needing others is equal to freedom. Depending on where those concepts have led you, it might be time for a reexamination, especially if your life hasn't unfolded to swimming in the warm azure waters of the Arabian Sea.

Let's look at this last one – independence equals freedom, and dependence equals the opposite. It's certainly one that has been a primary motivating force in our culture. Wealth has been presented as the path to independence, and out of dependence. The pursuit of wealth has eclipsed the pursuit of anything else. So let's look at that one.

Experience has shown that mankind is more disposed to suffer while evils are considered bearable, than to right themselves by abolishing the forms to which they are accustomed. If you don't know where those words are from maybe you know these: *We hold these truths to be self-evident, that all men are created equal, that they are endowed by their Creator with certain unalienable rights, that among . . .* That's right, The Declaration of Independence of the United States of America – the original document by which the concept of freedom was formed for us – the concept that freedom is independence. Whether you know it or not, whether you feel it or not, whether you believe it or not, you have adopted the concept that independence is freedom – when in actuality the opposite is true: the realization of *dependence* is the only true freedom, because there is no one who is independent of the energy that gives them life, that gives them breath.

We are all totally and absolutely dependent. The realization of that dependence is the only true freedom, because everything else is a fantasy. Everything else is something written in a guidebook about a beautiful beach, and we keep looking for the independence that is freedom – and it never is, because freedom is not independence. Freedom is the realization of complete dependence. Now these are words, and you could say, "Far out, yeah, cool, I dig it, I agree." – but the actual confrontation of this idea is profoundly disturbing, and nobody wants to think about it.

I want to tell you a story about the first time I remember thinking that there might be some credibility to the statement that *freedom is the realization of complete dependence*. Before that, as a kid, when my parents put restrictions on me, as all parents must do, “You can’t do this, you can’t do that,” my response of course was never, “Okay, thank you for not letting me . . .”

In my youth I had a summer job as a bellhop in a resort hotel in upstate New York. When I wasn’t working as a bellhop I would hang around the riding stables. It was a relatively upscale resort – not that I was upscale, but it was upscale. I liked to hang around the riding stables because that’s where the girls were. Until then I had ridden a horse only a couple of times, and never felt comfortable with it. I have an older sister who was good at it, and most of what she was good at I tried to avoid. Somehow, competing with her always turned out to be a losing deal.

So I didn’t ride, and the few times I tried it was scary. That certainly didn’t prevent me from hanging around the stables and pretending like I was comfortable there. After all, I knew I wouldn’t get up on a horse, and the girls were there. That is, until one day when there were some girls going out on a trail ride – I looked at the horses and thought foolishly, “I can do this.” They even asked me to come along. I couldn’t say no, or I didn’t want to say no, so I got up on the horse.

The short version of this story is: The horses started to gallop, everyone else was doing great, but I fell off. And what’s more, I didn’t want to get back on. I just didn’t want to get back on. So I took the coward’s way – I led the horse back to the stable. It was totally humiliating. Fortunately for me, this hotel had a brisk turnover of guests, so when these particular girls left at the end of the week, most, but not all of my humiliation ended.

I did come away with some resolve that this wasn't going to happen again – so I sought out Bill, the man in charge. He was British, and an accomplished trainer of show jumping horses. I asked if he would teach me, not merely how to ride, but to do all of it – jumping, training – all of it.

He was a very nice guy and we worked out an arrangement – but not before he said the following words to me: "The only chance you have to become a horseman is to do exactly what I tell you to do. You're not going to be able to do this without me." Hearing those words would certainly be a challenge, not only for any "I can do it myself" young man, but for anyone.

I wanted to learn, but I sure didn't like what he said. I remember where I was standing. I remember his face and the scene in which I heard the words, and for the first time had some recognition that it was true, "You are not going to be able to do this without me." So I went against my "I can do it myself" tendency to see him as someone who was restricting me from something, instead of recognizing that there were some steps that I had to take, before I was able to get what I wanted. He was generous and friendly, and I was intrigued by his demeanor – and of course, a new crop of girls were there. So when I wasn't working as a bellhop, I shoveled manure, practiced riding exercises, and did exactly what he told me.

Within a couple of months I got as good at being a horseman as one could in so short a time. I actually became competent enough around horses that the next spring I started working out thoroughbred race horses at Belmont Racetrack. I did that only for a short time, but I loved it. In the years between then and now, I have owned and ridden horses. He was right. I couldn't have done that without him. I was completely dependent on him.

All dependence is not something to be escaped from. Escape from all dependence is not independence, and it certainly is not peace. We are completely dependent on the force that gives us our breath. Whatever our perspective is – God, Nature, Physical laws, whatever – our life's breath is never our own. It always has to be given to us. There is not one breath that we take in our lives that we ourselves generate.

It would be like saying, "Okay breath, you've shown me how to do it, now I'll take it from here." Impossible! You can take it only as long as the time until the next breath, that's as long as you can take it. Once it stops giving us breath, we stop having breath. We are completely and absolutely dependent on the creative energy, on the force that generates life. We have no existence other than from that. If we are on a crusade to become independent, what is to stop us from forgetting that? Any moment that we are not in recognition of where our breath comes from, there is something missing.

If we come to imagine that we are generating our breath, how can we appreciate what we're given that proceeds from that breath – and everything we're given proceeds from that breath? People can be denied their sight and their hearing and still absorb impressions of life, but if a person is denied breath, they are denied life, and all of its manifestations.

Some people are so consumed with the insecurity of having to do something worthwhile, something creative, something worthy of attention, that life becomes nothing more than a series of frustrations. That quest comes from the insecurity that we will only be cared for if we are successful – but always there is that constant hand that is generating our breath, that constant energy that keeps everything going. If we were not so occupied with our independence, we might be able to feel that security.

Think of the wonderful feeling of really appreciating some help you've gotten, and saying thank you and meaning it, because you couldn't have done it yourself. It would be like that if it were for your breath. Thank you for that one, thank you for that one, and on and on and on. That would be a reflection of the feeling of the reality of being taken care of by something that feeds us breath by breath. Not day by day, not year by year, but breath by breath.

As life manifests, every time we get a breath, we're getting direct communication from the Creator saying, "I am here." Every time we get a breath we're getting that communication, as is everything that is getting breath along with us.

There are people that have gotten together to rediscover that connection, to find that peace. There is nothing wrong with seeking to become independent from things that cause you trouble. But when that seeking of independence causes us, as it will, to fail to remember our natural dependence, then we lose something much more precious.

Recognizing when our quest for independence has gone too far, requires extensive attention and exploration. Part of that exploration requires that we be receptive to experimenting with being in the position that I was in with Bill the horseman – a position that many people dedicate their lives to avoiding. If you wait for a metaphysical experience to become aware of the gift of breath – the gift of being dependent – that experience will pass you by. It is only available in the school of life, to those who are willing to explore being dependent.

Chapter 35
The Fishbowl

I was listening to a book on tape while driving home from Reno a few days ago. It wasn't a story I would recommend, but adequate as something to listen to while driving a road that I had driven many times. I eventually turned it off, but not before I tripped over a few minutes of a story that interested me.

Cheryl, who is a retired Vegas stripper, has saved enough money to own a bar. One of her employees – a waitress – wants to go to college, and is trying to save up enough money to do that. Cheryl tells her that the fastest way she's going to save money is not by waiting tables, even though she can do pretty well doing that, and maybe in a few years she can save enough money to go to college – but to swim in the glass tank behind the bar.

I've never seen that done in person, but I've seen it in movies or on TV, where in the back of the bar there's a glass tank, and there's a girl in a bikini swimming around. Back to the story. When the waitress asks how much money she'd make swimming around in the tank, Cheryl tells her that she'd make three times as much as waiting tables. She pays the girls a lot, because they have to stay under water for a couple of hours at a time getting air from a pipe down in the wall of the tank. The tank was the major attraction of the bar, and Cheryl had trouble getting girls to do that.

When the waitress says that she doesn't think she wants to be that kind of an attraction, Cheryl reminds her how much she likes having people think she's pretty, and is always getting dressed up when she isn't waitressing. "Yeah, but not constantly . . . like it would be in a fish tank." Then she said, "I wouldn't want to live in a fish bowl."

You know that expression, "to live in a fish bowl?" I turned off my book on tape after I heard that expression. I knew that I heard something important, and wanted to think about it. I've been thinking about that quote for the last few days, and I realized that this was the reason that the path that I teach is so unpopular. Our rate of increase is about what you'd make in a non-interest checking account – about a dollar a year, no matter how much money you deposit – and our attrition rate, which means the opposite, is fairly considerable.

I think this idea of living in a fish bowl is the reason, because, *who wants to live in a fish bowl?* How about the famous quote from the De Niro gangster movie, "What are *you* lookin' at, you lookin' at *me*?" That must reflect that somebody is looking at you when you don't want to be looked at. If you wanted to be looked at you wouldn't say, "What are *you* lookin' at?"

There are a lot of moments when you don't want to be looked at. In fact, most people, in most moments, don't want to be looked at. Every once in a while, when you put a lot of energy into your appearance, or some presentation you have to make as a sales person, you want to be looked at, because that's what you've *prepared* for. But all the rest of the time you don't want that.

When we see the red carpet at the Academy Awards, we see examples of the amount of preparation people put into their personal appearance so as to be comfortable living in *that* fish bowl. You can tell how insecure those people really are about their appearance – they have to do so much to be okay to be seen in public. In those moments, they want to be looked at. They are walking down the red carpet and the photographers are snapping their picture, but most of the time they don't want to live in a fish bowl, and would need a very good reason to do so.

That's why some people find it so challenging to be involved with a teacher. They may try for a while, but when they begin to recognize that living an examined life is required – and not only that *you* have to examine your life, but other people are going to be examining your life too, we hear, "I don't think so. That's like living in a fish bowl." It's not attractive, it's even intimidating for people to live a life that's going to be examined, not only by themselves, which is a big thing, but by other people as well.

I knew a professional golfer who hired a few golfing instructors when he was having trouble with his swing. He had them come with him when he was practicing. He had them stand north, south, east, and west around him while he was hitting his driver. By having them stand in front, behind, left, and right of him while watching his swing, he would be living an examined life in relation to his golf swing.

He recognized that no matter how much he examined his swing, he wouldn't have the perspective that the person on the right, or maybe the person on the left, or the front, or the back would have, and he needed that perspective. He sought out that perspective enough that he solicited people to keep an eye on him in those moments, so he could learn what he had to learn about the defect in his swing that was causing his trouble. In that limited case, he valued *living in a fishbowl.*

What is this discord that keeps us from the freedom that we suspect is possible – that keeps us from the peace that we suspect is possible? We're reluctant to examine our lives in a way necessary to find out what's actually going on. We are very reluctant to put ourselves in that position. We're rarely even willing to ask those questions, but what it takes to answer those questions is another thing. To live an examined life refers not only to our personal lives, but to examine the nature of life in our time, and in our place, in order to discover what's going on. What's gone wrong here?

Maybe you've heard that meditation is the ultimate, so you want to do that. You don't want to do the beginning stuff. You want to do the advanced stuff. That's the American way, and in some things, it's possible. It's possible to get foods that are frozen, and after you defrost them, you have the original product. It's possible to go to a restaurant and have something with fifteen ingredients made, put on a plate, and you get to eat it right there.

But in the spiritual pursuit, it's not possible. What needs to be done is the refinement of being, starting from exactly where you are, and who you are, not who you imagine yourself to be, not who you would like people to think you are, but exactly who you are. If you're restless and you can't concentrate unless something concentrates you –

that's who you are. You may be able to watch a movie that hits you over the head, but if you can't watch a movie that is subtle, and you can't read a book that is subtle, and you can't hear explanations that are subtle, then that's who you are. If black and white is no good, if it's got to be color, if repetition is no good, if it's got to have variety, then that's who you are, and that's where you have to begin.

If you get to know yourself clearly, you'll know the coarseness that is there. Your imagination that you're going to move from that state of coarseness to meditation is your imagination. The vibration of actual meditation starts at a very fine place. It doesn't start at the altitude of ordinary life. It starts at a much finer point – a point where there is no blame, no self-pity, no excuses, no restlessness and rushing, or at least very little of all those things.

So our effort in the beginning has to go toward refining our state of being. As much as you would like to learn advanced exercises, you first have to see yourself as you are, and start from that place. And you need a support system of other people who are willing to admit where they are at, and not putting on an act that we're all spiritual, and we're all calling ourselves brothers and sisters, when we can barely call our own brothers and sisters, brother and sister. That is where we have to start, and refine, and refine, and refine, and release – release what you see as not productive anymore.

The other day I was at a house across the road in the woods. There are a whole bunch of wild turkeys there. Unfortunately for the turkeys, there's also a family of coyotes that live in the area. Obviously the coyotes watch the turkeys – they're something to eat. I was looking out the window and saw a coyote about 100 ft. away. He didn't look like he was getting ready to charge – maybe just assessing the situation – maybe he'd just eaten a turkey and wasn't hungry. I don't have that kind of knowledge to be able to assess that. I was just watching. I don't want some Wild Kingdom carnage to take place in front of me; I'd prefer it take place in the back of the food market. Here were these beautiful turkeys, one even with his fan spread out. So I figure I'll put myself in between the turkeys and the coyote, because a coyote isn't going to mess with a person. They are actually fairly small.

I walked out the door and started to edge the coyote in one direction, and the turkeys started going in that direction also. I couldn't explain to the turkeys, "You fuckin' turkey, you're going the wrong way! You're moving right toward the coyote." What could I do? So I was chasing the coyotes, and the turkeys think they're being chased, and they all took off into the woods together. I didn't see how the rest of the drama played out, but what an interesting situation, and what a parallel we have here.

What if someone told you that they could get between you and your coyotes – the coyotes that keep you in whatever situation you're repeating and repeating – the coyotes that keep you from experiencing the peace and harmony that has eluded you? What if someone told you that they could help you do that, and you even knew enough about that person to think that it could be possible? If you solicited their help, and they moved toward you with just a question, where would *you* go? Would you run toward your coyotes? People do. Hard to believe, those dumb turkeys. But people do move away from help and towards their coyotes; they think they're avoiding emotional pain and discomfort.

We certainly understand that physical pain and discomfort is an indicator. If we didn't have these, we could get a ruptured appendix and die. If we didn't have pain and discomfort, things could happen to us that couldn't be cured, because we wouldn't know we had the affliction. Physical indications of pain and discomfort can be a gift, because they are notifying us that something is wrong. If we're mistreating our bodies, if we're smoking cigarettes, our lungs may hurt, we may be short of breath. If it weren't for pain and discomfort, we might smoke cigarettes and die a premature death and not know why. So pain and discomfort are gifts, or can be gifts.

It's relatively easy to acknowledge that physical pain and discomfort can be gifts, but our interpretation of emotional pain and discomfort, is that they are a curse. Is it possible that emotional pain and discomfort are also gifts? Our ordinary interpretation is very clear. Pain is pain and discomfort is discomfort, and they should be eliminated – especially when they're emotional. But what if they were our gift to learn about some discord in us? What if that was the case? Then our ordinary interpretation would be self-destructive, just like ignoring an appendix pain would be.

Chapter 36
The Gopis

This book includes many unique ideas, important ideas. It formulates new and exciting perspectives, and alludes to disciplines and methods. It documents what's wrong with us – that we're in prison, and we need to get free. All these cerebral components of our efforts toward freedom are critical, but focusing excessively on them can produce an unbalanced picture. I know this, because my early years of spiritual seeking were consumed with pursuits of the mind – that is, until good fortune played a trick on me.

If you had met me forty years ago you would have met a self-assured young man. Though I had lived in New York City for most of my life, and had the hubris that went along with those particular roots, I had also absorbed a spiritual and psychological foundation. This combination of influences that formed me, created what you might call an arrogant spiritual attitude.

A man whom I had met some years before, had taken an interest in my well-being. (I describe more about this relationship elsewhere in the book.) He suggested that I spend some time in seclusion in a place set up for that purpose in central Asia. I ended up spending an extended period of time in this isolated situation, and it had a profound effect on me. It was difficult sometimes, but I learned to be by myself far better than I had before. For one hundred days I never saw another person.

When that was over, I was supposed to go to north-eastern Afghanistan to meet that same man who had arranged my retreat. I eventually met him, and after spending several weeks together, I headed for Delhi, India, to catch my flight back to the U.S.

I had no particular reason to be in Delhi – I just wanted to fly home from there. I had an open ticket and had to arrange a date to fly. As it turned out, the flights were booked up for the next five days. I decided to spend those days in India as young foreigners commonly did at that time.

After making a few inquiries, I ran into the information I was looking for. "Why don't you come with us? We're going to an ashram. It's free. They'll put you up and they have great food." There were a lot of American "freaks" going around looking for a place to find themselves. I didn't put myself in that category because I already had spiritual roots, but I was in that category whether I put myself there or not.

I went along with my new-found friends, and we ended up in an ashram. The food and the accommodations were great. That's always a decent reason to stay around, because sometimes accommodations can be pretty basic. Sometimes you have to sleep on a concrete floor and eat yogurt and lentils every day. But at this place they took good care of people in a way that made it attractive for me to stay. Oh yeah – and the girls were beautiful. I had no particular spiritual interest in them because they were twenty and twenty-one years old, and after the profundity of my retreat, I couldn't conceive of possibly learning anything from them.

They were of the Gopi variety – very sweet and devotional – looking like they could do no wrong. But to me they looked like . . . you know, like the wolf and . . . like that. I don't think I was unusually lecherous, but the spiritual priorities of a young guy can be inconsistent, and I was certainly not numb to that type of attraction, especially after a hundred days of seclusion – spiritual or otherwise.

There I was, in an ashram. During the day I could do whatever I wanted. So that's when I did my flirting around. At night, every night, they had programs that lasted from about 6:00 to 10:00 pm. After that we would sing devotional songs till maybe 11:00pm, 12:00 or 1:00 am.

I found myself going along with the routine. It was mildly entertaining, even though I wasn't really curious about what was going on there spiritually. When the time came to leave, I called up to confirm my plane reservation, and there was no seat for me. They said my ticket had expired. In the U.S. you can always work that out. But in a foreign country, especially India, which is fairly chaotic, it's not like, "Oh well, no problem."

It *was* a problem. I went into Haridwar, the nearest town, but didn't get anything confirmed, except that I didn't have a flight, and it was going to be two weeks till I would have one. I tried all the New York-type things I knew, but they just weren't working.

I was going to be there for two weeks, and I could either spend the two weeks at the airline counter waiting for a flight to come up sooner, or I could go back to the ashram, where I knew I would be welcome. So I went back.

Of course now I was in an entirely different position. You see, it wasn't one of those ashrams where there are thousands of people. There were hundreds, but there weren't thousands. So when I came back, it was like, "Oh, he's coming back for more! Now he's serious. Now he's really interested. Now he's one of us." You get the picture? I tried to make it very clear that was not the case, but they were not receptive to my interpretation of my circumstances. In their interpretation, it was the Grace of the Guru that brought me back, not the lack of seats on the airline.

I knew that if I were going to be there for two weeks, I had to get into the spiritual scene, even though the sweetness of the environment wore on me. I was a little bit coarse when it came to matters of the heart, but I still was attuned to the spiritual sense of things. I knew there was something going on there, although it was not something that was necessarily attractive to me.

Even though I made feeble attempts at assimilation, the circumstances remained that I was *here* . . . and *they* . . . you know who *they* are (everybody else), they were *there*. I was here, and they were there, and what's more – I wasn't about to go over to *there*.

I considered myself pretty convincing and dynamic – an intelligent young guy. My thought was to bring some of them over to my side. My idea was that I would explain to them, *Sure, this is all very beautiful, but let's think about it for a second. Let's analyze this for a second.* So I chose a couple of likely candidates, whose intention, of course, was to draw me into *their* circle. Since my intention was to draw *them* out of *their* circle, I would bring up little contradictions, or mention interesting observations. As it turned out, when I made my move, all that happened was they would look at me with those beatific innocent faces and say, "Just forget about that and open up your heart. Just forget about your thoughts and ideas, and surrender your mind." I'd say, "Sure, I can go along with that. But how about this? But how about that?" And they'd say, "Just forget about that – it's all mind."

One of the girls told me, that when she had first arrived there she had so many questions and so much confusion. Now she saw it was all a product of thinking. "Just give up your mind," she advised. Of course this was not a reasonable request to someone whose mind was very much what they depended on. The concept of giving up my mind was not, "Oh, yeah! Let's go for it." It wasn't like that at all.

So the days went on and on, and I kept trying to win converts but wasn't getting anywhere. Still, every night I would go to the *satsang* program, because what else was I going to do? I found myself sitting there and listening to people speaking in English and singing songs in Hindi. During the day, when I would talk with the girls, they would say, "Just come to the program tonight and sooner or later you'll understand." And of course I would come to the program, not so much to understand, but because I didn't have anything else to do – and we did sing beautiful music.

A week went by, and one day I was sitting with a few people trying again to sell my mind-stuff. One of the girls said, "You know, there's a guy here that you really have to talk to. He's from the U.S. In fact, he's even from the East Coast and he's really smart. I think he was a lawyer or something like that. You've got to meet Harry. You'll be able to ask him all your questions."

I said to myself, "All right, now I'm set. I'll have a person to talk to, and we can talk about *them* together." It wasn't hard to find this guy, and when I eventually did, I introduced myself, and told him that I was from New York. After I put forth a few of my better observations, Harry looked at me with a non-New York smile, waited a few moments, and said, "When I first came here I was like that too. Forget about all that, just give up your mind and open up your heart."

At that moment there was no refuge left for my resistance. I both freaked out and opened up at the same time. I knew there was no hope of escape. When you go to a foreign country you're pretty much there. It's not like, "Well, I'll be out of here in a few minutes." I knew that there was something going on there – not only because of this guy Harry, but from being exposed to all of it, and seeing those twenty-year-old girls with beatific smiles wearing white and singing and being in love. Even with as much cynicism as I carried around with me, I didn't have that much self-deception that I could say that there was nothing going on there. I knew there was something going on there – something that I knew nothing about.

Little by little my thoughts began to mellow. I began to see that scene as special, but I retained the arrogant conviction, that if only they had my expanded view of spirituality, it would round out the whole picture for them. Eventually I began to understand what I was there to receive, and what they had to offer me. It was not until my last day there, however, that I realized that they really didn't need what I had to offer them.

After spending a few weeks at the ashram, I did eventually take my plane home, but to this day I know that missing my flight in India was instrumental in learning a valuation for an open heart. This event really changed my estimation of what can be experienced through thoughts, which is considerable, what can be experienced through sensations, which is considerable, what can be experienced through feelings, which is considerable, and what can be experienced through an open heart and the love that it allows – which is unlimited.

If you wish to be a master,
I can't help you.
I was taught by servants.
They taught me how to serve.
If you wish to be a magician,
There I can't help you either.
I was taught by heroes.
They taught me how to save.
And this also I was taught:
Chance to open up your senses
To the universe that touches you
For it will fill you up with its myriad sensations.
Chance to open up your mind
To the universe of intelligence
For it will fill you up with its myriad ideas.
Chance to open up your heart
To the universe of emotions
For it will fill you up with its myriad feelings.
These things I was taught.
And yes, one more thing.

As a servant is filled,
Only a small bit of what is collected can be kept,
And a hero even less.
But to this law there is one exception.
If you open up your heart to the universe of love,
It will fill you up completely.

I want you to know that I wrote this poem. Not that it's important that I wrote it, but it's important for you to know that's the way I look at things. I want to remind you of something I told you earlier about myself, and sometimes a poem can reflect a facet of a person that a narrative can't. It is my belief, and my experience, that whatever else a person does, however they apply themselves, there is really nothing that has that taste of an open heart – nothing. In these times that we're living, it may be more difficult for us to consider opening our hearts. It may almost seem alien, maybe even dangerous, but until we taste that open heart, how can we really know what it is that we seek?

So if we seek mastery, or mystery, or magic, or transcendence, or self-discipline, or we seek eternal life – until we know how much we might receive from having an open heart, how can we know that we really want to pursue those things? It may be that a lot of our dissatisfaction will be calmed with the discovery of that open heart. It may be that our seeking is motivated by our ideas, and our thoughts, and our concepts, and our fears, and our desire to control the events of our lives. With the calm that comes from an open heart, and the filled-up-ness that comes from an open heart, we might not find ourselves to be such fervent seekers of those other things.

I can say that because when I was young, I learned something from those twenty-year-old Gopis who wouldn't discuss any spiritual concepts with me, because they were in the process of opening up their hearts to the universe of love so they could be filled up by it.

A while after I'd returned home from India, I began to suspect that there was something missing in me. It was scary to think about, but there was something cracking. Of course, my worst fear was, *Am I going to become one of them*? And you know what? I did become one of them, and I am one of them. That is the feeling in my heart. I have as much affinity for those Gopis as I do for any other spiritual interaction I have ever had in my life. Yes, I am a teacher of methods of achieving consciousness, but I am a slave to an open heart. And that, as far as I'm concerned, is the only way to go.

Chapter 37
Devotion

It's interesting the incidental things we remember for years, and in this case, years and years. I went hiking in the desert with several of my friends. On the way home I was trying to remember what foods were in the refrigerator for my post-camping eating frenzy. We were traveling in two separate cars, and one car stopped for dinner at an all-you-can-eat buffet on the way back. I wanted to know what was in my refrigerator, because the people in my car didn't want to stop, and I certainly didn't feel like going food shopping. I was sure some of my favorites were in there because I'd bought extras anticipating the state I'd be in when I returned from camping.

When I got home, my second stop was at the refrigerator. I opened it up and my treats weren't there. All afternoon I had been proceeding with the assumption that they were there. Of course I was disappointed – my assumption was incorrect, and clouded by the way I wanted things to be.

What would be your next step if you could temporarily accept the possibility that your assumptions were sometimes erroneous, unfounded, and certainly unexamined? To begin with, you would have to try to develop a certain flexibility. How else could you be open to discovering that your conclusions about life might be biased? How else could you be open to discovering that you arrive at your conclusions because of a need to see things in a predetermined way? If I didn't want those treats to be in the refrigerator as much as I did, I might have remembered correctly that they weren't there.

In acquiring that flexibility, you might then be able to look at some of the concepts that you've developed about life; what's good, what's not good, what's important, what's basic, what's standard equipment, and what you wouldn't be okay without. I'm not suggesting that somebody else make judgments about your conception of how life should be, but for you to re-examine those unexamined concepts – those assumptions. Then you can reasonably decide what's okay with you and what isn't. Is your view of the world actually how it is? If you are operating under illusion, do you want to maintain that illusion?

The particular example I want to discuss is the concept and assumption about what's been called *devotion.* Anyone who has researched, or even generally approached the subject of spiritual progress, expansion of consciousness, or the quest for inner freedom has, in their reading or in meeting other people, run into the historical concept of devotion. That person has adopted a viewpoint about this idea of devotion from their schooling, their learning and development, their programming, or some exposure that took place sometime in their past.

But what is the actual nature of devotion? Let's begin with how we come to see it in a distorted way – that distortion making it almost impossible to assimilate it into our lives, or if we do assimilate it, we do so in a distorted way.

If you were coming home and expecting something to be in your refrigerator and it wasn't, your concept would be incorrect, and you would suffer because of it. People have concepts about what it means to be devoted to something, and those concepts often generate misunderstanding. People imagine they are participating in devotion, and what they think is happening is not happening. They may be participating in an illusion, like imagining a feeling of devotion to God. Unfortunately, that concept is so far beyond a human capacity, that although it may be a convenient devotion, it is not an actual devotion. It's a fanciful emotion.

The progression to real devotion starts with something relatively close to you – something that you can easily recognize, something that you can see, something that actually and tangibly affects you. As you travel the path of that devotion it may expand, and at some point, you may experience and feel a true devotion to the supreme power that creates and generates the breath of your life.

But at this stage your concept of devotion to God is imaginary, and will not lead to that true devotion. Similarly, your devotion and singing to Krishna, or anyone you never actually knew, and are never going to know, is the same.

Devotional music may be lovely and sound beautiful, but if you aren't singing it to someone real to you, it will at best be a *feel good*, and at worst, be an illusion that obstructs any real devotion.

It may make you feel good, but so many things can make you feel good. Some people feel good getting spun around in a ride at an amusement park. Of course the net benefit from that is, it shakes you up, and makes you feel like you are alive, but then it re-deposits you in your life, and all you feel is nauseated.

If you are devoted to your job, your performance is very different than if you only do it for the money, and then go home. If you are devoted to your family, then your attitude towards them is very different than if you're not. If you are devoted to your friends, those who help you, your actions are so much different than if you take their care for granted. So we can see that devotion is a very wonderful, encouraging, supplementing, and enlivening force. But it is always devotion *to* something. Otherwise people are either not feeling devotion, or imagining that they are feeling devotion by doing something to feel good, and helping pass the time in a way that's attractive.

If you feel any of those practical and actual devotions, you are on the path to spiritual devotion. They are elementally connected. The only difference is in the object of devotion – and that will evolve as you do.

Chapter 38
Surprise

I learned how to play poker as a very young boy. Of course, I didn't start out playing for money. My first exposure to gambling at poker was actually strip poker. I was in junior high school, and that's the kind of crowd I hung with. Do you know how strip poker goes? You play a hand, and the loser takes off an article of clothing. When you get down to a certain level, the stakes have obviously gone up. I remember a strip poker game where we were getting down to that level, when somebody lost the next hand and said, "I ain't doin' it." It was probably a guy, because the girls were always a little more . . . the girls I knew, anyway. So he said, "I ain't doin' it." So somebody else said, "Well, I'll take off mine, if you take off yours."

That's what I'm saying to you – *I'll take off mine if you take off yours*. That's the admission price. That's it. If you won't agree, you'll have snuck in, and you know how it is when you sneak in. When I was a kid, sometimes we snuck into the movies, and most of the time we weren't able to watch the movie, because we were so busy making sure we didn't get caught.

You want to get somewhere you haven't gone to before. You don't want more of what you know; you already have plenty of that. You want to go beyond that into what you don't know. That's where the magic is, where the beauty is. There's something you may know a little about, but you want to know more, or there's something you may have experienced a little, but you want to experience more. That's where you want to go to – someplace unknown – someplace a little bit unfamiliar.

If you want to get to someplace unknown and unfamiliar, there may have to be some decisions that are made for you – you can't make them yourself. If you make them yourself, you probably will make them the way you made them before, and that won't take you to someplace unknown. It'll take you to someplace that you've known before. It will take you to someplace that you're familiar with, that you're comfortable with. It won't be deeper, it won't be higher, it won't be more beautiful, it won't be further. It will be more of what you already have.

It's not that you have to throw out all your decisions and priorities, but you may have to allow in one or two new elements. I call that surprise, because in the moment that a new element comes in, there is always a little bit of surprise. It's a little bit of, "whoa!" – like, *I'll take off mine if you take off yours*. When has a sentence like that ever been used in a book of this kind? Never in a spiritual book. So there's a little surprise there. It's a delightful surprise for those of you who don't feel it as threatening. You feel you are in someplace new. It's a feeling like, "Oh, there's a little difference here." It may be a little unsettling because, *if we're going to go there, where are we going to go next*? Of course you always have the option to say no. In matters of surprise, things should always proceed slowly, and always with volunteers, never with victims. Even when surprises are small, they can be impactful, because everything else we have is what *we* set up.

Unfortunately, when we are surprised by some circumstance, we usually try to eliminate the surprise element, by making it into something we know, or else we leave, we withdraw. Alive dynamics come in the moments between being surprised, and effectively eliminating that surprise by covering it up. That's it; that's life. All the rest is repetition. You may have variables on a certain theme – you live here, then you live there – you do this, and then you do that, but *you* are always there, *you* are the constant, and *different* doesn't happen, because *you* can't make different happen.

You're going around on a Ferris wheel and there's a funny noise, then it stops. And suddenly you're *there*. You're right there. The Ferris wheel was nice – it was pleasant, but now for a moment you feel super alive. So you start to discuss it. "This happens all the time. It'll get going in a moment." You try to eliminate the element of surprise, even though it's the most alive moment you've had all day! And that's even a physical, graphic, kind of coarse example. How about turning at the end of a supermarket aisle and bumping into someone you really didn't want to see? That's a surprise. How do you handle that one? What would you do to regain your footing? How would you eliminate that surprise? If you could (which you probably can't), you would pretend that you didn't even see them.

It's really important to understand that *change* is based on surprise. It's based on having small moments that you don't control completely, as you seek to do in all your other moments. Change requires that you relax your desire to control each small thing, so that you can't always predict each next moment of your life.

Can you acknowledge that your life hasn't been alive enough, that you would want it to go on exactly as it has been for an equal number of years into your future? You probably wouldn't want that repetition, even if you could have a bigger house, and a different husband or wife, or whatever it would be for you. You'd want more depth, you'd want something more real.

Of course you've been the architect of what you have. It hasn't been done *to* you – you've made the choices. You haven't made them freely, but you've made them. You've created the world around you, and that world will be replicated in your next years, unless some other element unexpectedly enters – and that requires surprise. Wherever you go, there you are; wherever you go, the architect goes with you. You know that in nature. You know that in your refrigerator. You know that with your car, but you don't yet know that with yourself.

You hope that some miracle is going to come in and suspend the laws of repetition for no reason whatsoever. Fortunately, the laws of repetition *can* be suspended, but *not* for no reason whatsoever. It would require you being in an environment where a new element could come into your life that wasn't there before. You cannot surprise yourself. You cannot.

If you have the *nobody's gonna tell me what to do* attitude, then how will you make use of that element of surprise? When you're surprised, you usually feel the need to defend and protect yourself, in order to make the surprise go away. So if somebody asks, "Hey, what are you doing?" you have the urge to say, "Nothing. There's nothing happening. There's nothing to see here." You feel like somebody has opened the window and said, "Let's take a look at this," but all you want to do is close it. Maybe it's like one of those sticky windows, and you're trying all your tricks to close it. "What did you say? I didn't hear that," or, "Oh yeah, I do that all the time. It's not what you think, I know what you're thinking, but it's not what it looks like!"

Someone has given you the opportunity to have that moment of life, that moment of surprise. What a gift. It doesn't matter what their motivation for saying something might be, or what they're thinking, or what they know, or what they don't know. There's always an open window, especially if you can look with a little perspective. The longer the window is open, the more possibilities you have. The more quickly the window is closed, the less possibilities you have.

Can you imagine loving open windows? Can you imagine recognizing their value, their necessity? If you don't develop an affinity for being surprised – if you don't develop a valuation for being surprised, those wonderfully dangerous experiences will be relegated to your imagination.

Chapter 39

Climbing & Resting

Have you ever climbed a really high mountain? If you have, you know that once you get started, you don't just keep climbing and climbing and climbing. Every once in a while, you stop and rest. If your mountain is a popular climbing spot, there will even be certain places that are prescribed stops. It might be a little level spot on which you have just enough room to pitch a tent. When you get to one of these spots you can actually stop and rest, cook and eat. If it's big enough, you can even hang out there for a while. But sooner or later you'd probably want to climb on. Then again you might not.

When we start off on the spiritual path, we want to learn to climb to a new height and gain a more expanded perspective. After we've climbed for a while we begin to feel tired. We feel it's time for a rest. After all, we're already above the height of the plains. We feel good about ourselves.

We feel a little stronger. We're not such a leaf-in-the-wind as we once were, and it feels good. Even if you only climb to the first base camp, you've accomplished something. You're already above everyone who hasn't, everyone in the whole world who hasn't.

You've earned a rest. You could take a short rest then resume your climb. But if you don't resume it soon, you could find that you've permanently set up your tent there. If something doesn't call your attention to the length of your rest, you might even find yourself building a cabin and making a life there. As long as you don't associate with the people who are climbing on, you'll never feel dissatisfied, you'll never call it what it is – an overextended rest stop. Of course when climbers come through camp, it's going to feel a little disquieting. Since you're resting and they're going on, it will be upsetting to associate with them, so you'll have to do something to separate yourself from them.

You can deceive yourself into feeling strong if you surround yourself with people who have not climbed as far as you have. You are in good shape compared to them, but you are not in good shape compared to everyone.

Anyone who has made some efforts, and climbed to a certain height, realizes that there is a lot more to learn then they thought. The mountains are higher than they imagined. *It's a long way to the top if you wanna rock and roll.* It's going to be a long, steep climb. It's attractive to rest from time to time. When you rest, you don't have to exert. René Daumal wrote in Mount Analogue, "Never halt on a shifting slope." That is amazing advice if you really let it in, because all these places where we think we're setting up camp to rest, they are all on shifting slopes. They may not be shifting rapidly, but they are shifting, and sooner or later, as he says, "The gravel will begin to slip imperceptibly, and suddenly it will drop away under you and launch you like a ship." But it won't launch you right away. You might be seventy years old before you find out that you had been launched. You wouldn't want that to happen, to find yourself having been launched like a ship. So, I recommend that unless you're ready to set up a permanent camp, and call it quits on the climbing, you make sure that some of the time you are hanging out with bigger dogs than you – ones who are still going up the mountain.

Chapter 40

Vamos a Ver Que Pasa

My daughter is thirty years old now and lives in New York City, but when she was about three, we lived out in the country. I have a son who's a couple of years older than she; he was a quiet, almost contemplative child, but she was a squirmer. I called her the human worm – very curious and always getting into things. With kids that are like that, you have to be a little more attentive, because you don't know what they're going to do next. Some things that you don't want them to get into are obvious, and other things, like climbing trees, maybe yes, maybe no, but some things are a clear *no*.

We had one of those double ovens with a glass front, where the bottom one was really low, and she could reach it. She would try to put her hand on the glass door of the oven when there was something cooking, and you know what the result of that would be. So I had to explain to her that there's this law, this rule, the way that it is, that human hands cannot go on a very hot surface without doing damage.

It's like when a very big object comes in contact with a very small object, the small object is going to pay the price, not the big object. So don't walk out into the street, because there are a lot of big objects there – things like that, things that we as adults take for granted. We are all prepared and willing to pass those lessons on to our children, and to others who may need that instruction.

But what if there were laws, or *ways that it is* of which you are unaware, and the understanding of those laws, or *ways that it is* has eluded you? You can't pass them on. You can't teach them. I know we'd like to think that there are no such things, and that we are free of all the laws, other than those placed on us by our fellow humans. Yes, we can drive without our license in our pocket, and probably not get caught, and maybe even drive without a license altogether, and still not get caught. We can evade and circumvent many of the laws made by humans, but there are some things that we cannot circumvent.

We recognize that there is something called gravity, and if we're on a ladder and we slip and fall, we're going to end up on the ground, not on top of the ladder. We know that, and don't question it – but there are other laws that affect us that we don't know about. Since we don't know about them, our actions can be misdirected in the same way as the ladder example. If the ladder is high you'll be injured, if you put your hand on the hot glass door you will get burnt, and if you step out in the street when a car is coming, you will not hurt the car, the car will hurt you.

When the astronauts were first developing the technology to go into space, there were certain things they needed. Obviously they needed to work out their food, their bathroom situation, how they would get around in the spaceship or module, etc. Another thing they had to work out was how they would take notes – how they would write down the things that had to be recorded. So they contracted a technology research team for $3.5 million to develop a pen that would work in zero gravity, and was not susceptible to breaking down. It took months to develop, but in the end they were very proud of their zero-gravity pen.

One of the astronauts brought a pen home to show his six-year-old kid, and tried to explain what they had developed, and how incredible American technology was. The six-year-old looked at the pen and asked, “Why couldn’t you use a pencil?” That is a true story.

I recognize that the nature of our lives is that we have come to appreciate complexity. We respect complexity. Anything too simple has to be deficient. That’s why there are so many different things on the shelves of the supermarket – because there must be a better way, there must be a different way, there must be some combination of things that improves on the last combination of things. We’re always looking for the new wrinkle.

I know we have that disease, because we are part of a culture that has that disease. It makes it harder to appreciate something simple – even an idea. Ideas have to be embellished and stirred together in an interesting and entertaining way for them to be appreciated. Somewhere in there, there’s the essence of the story, but the story has to be more complicated than a Zen koan. We've slipped a long way into complexity from *the water is wet*.

For many years I knew a man whose opinions and presence I valued very much. These writings would not exist had I not crossed paths with him. At one point he made a suggestion that I go out and see if I could pass on some of what I'd learned, and what I understood. I asked him what the point would be, and what I would be trying to accomplish. Although he lived in South America, he spoke English fluently, but this time he answered my question with the Spanish expression, *Vamos a ver que pasa*, which means, let's see what happens.

Of course I wanted more information than *let's see what happens.* My idea for myself wasn't that I would be a teacher, or a guru, or anything like that. I had spent years getting used to being okay with myself, and I thought that was pretty cool, because before that, I had been restless and manipulative. I felt at peace with myself for the first time, and now he was suggesting that I go out and do this – so I wanted to know why.

I certainly followed his suggestion, even though I never got more explanation than *vamos a ver que pasa.* I put my picture on posters, and people came to meetings that I held at the University of Oregon. I talked once each week, and a group of people formed that eventually moved out to the farm where I was living with my kids and the double oven. I did this for a few years, and we explored some really interesting things.

It was about this time that he made another suggestion – that I put my group aside for a year or so, and check out a newly-formed spiritual group that was evoking a lot of interest. When I asked him why I would be doing that (which were of course the magic words) he said, "*Vamos a ver que pasa.*" I tried to get more information about his idea for me, and he said a little something more. But I was left with following his suggestion, and really trying to get enveloped in this group, watching what happened, and seeing what observations I could make. I did that for more than a year.

After that, I had the opportunity to put an idea into motion based on my own *vamos a ver que pasa.* I wanted to take six to eight people on a big converted school bus/motor home and drive around the country to places where non-traditional spiritual ideas barely existed; places like Montana and Idaho, and small towns where the wave of California spirituality had not reached. I wanted to see what it would be like to present people with a simple form of the idea that there is something called meditation, and self-study. I was curious enough to see what would happen and, a few months later, we found ourselves in Mountain Home, Idaho.

We carried an entertaining half-hour long spiritual movie with us, and played music and talked. We would roll into a new town, and set up a program in a free venue of some kind. It was a total everyman situation – farmers, garage mechanics, school teachers, fast food workers, even off-duty soldiers, if there was a base nearby. We'd play music, and talk, and show this movie, and see how it went . . . you know, *vamos a ver que pasa*.

People in the town would find out that we'd be having a program because we would put up posters. We also went to the local newspaper, and radio, and TV stations. We'd park our bus outside so they could come onboard and interview us – and they did. One time we went to a radio station in

Helena, Montana, and a redneck guy who announced crop yields on his program came on the bus to interview us. We talked to him on the air, and he asked some good questions. At the end he announced where our program would be, and added, "So, let's go – let's see what happens!" He said it in English with a country twang, but it seemed to come from the same place as the last *vamos a ver que pasa* I heard.

This radio announcer came into contact with something completely different from his ordinary life, something he had no frame of reference for. He asked us questions like, "Well, is it like this? Is it like that?" He couldn't fit it in anywhere, so he went back to the place where the kid said, "Why couldn't you use a pencil?" It was not a complicated analysis for him, so this very spontaneous and natural thing came out – *let's see what happens.* That had a huge impact on me – how natural and just beneath the surface our experimental attitude is about life.

There is something beneath all the protections and all the complexity that has been added onto us, and we've somehow been complicit in letting that happen. No, not consciously, but innocently. In our quest for safety, to get noticed, to be loved – all these things have conspired to eliminate the simplicity of *let's see what happens,* to the point that it's gone from our existence. It's not there anymore. So we end up manipulating everything we do. We can leave nothing alone. In the moment, we feel compelled to change whatever we see, so that it's the way that we think it should be, the way we want it to be, the way we need it to be, rather than – *let's see what happens*. When you venture out, whether it be to do something you do every day, or something you rarely do, there is no *vamos a ver que pasa.* There is only *this is the way I want it to work out.*

What if there were a law, not a rule set up by people, but a law like gravity – that the natural state of a human being is that state of curiosity that doesn't have a determined picture of the way it should be? What if that law affected us, and we were subject to that law, even if we fought against it?

You know what it's like to fight against a law. You have to have meetings. You have to raise money, and have placards – and that's only for a political law. Resisting a fundamental law is like rowing a raft upstream. I tried that in Costa Rica with a dugout log canoe that must have weighed 5,000 lbs. We were paddling and paddling, just to stay in the same place, not end up down river somewhere in the jungle.

If you're going against a fundamental law, your life is going to be constant struggle. Nobody is going to be acceptable to you, no place where you are is going to be acceptable to you. Everything is going to require some manipulation on your part. That's what it's going to be like if you're fighting against a fundamental law.

What if the entity that we call the human race is actually an experiment? What if the design of human life was concocted and manifested in order to – *vamos a ver que pasa* – to see what happens? I'm not talking about some *overmind* that's having this idea. I'm talking about an energy that can conceive of this without having to think it up. Maybe it's a natural progression of that energy to create experiments, and we are part of those experiments, but we don't recognize that it is an experiment, or that we are an experiment. So the events of our lives are not looked on as "*let's see what happens.*" It's not *let's you and me sign these papers and go live together and see what happens.* It's called marriage. Can you imagine . . . let's go into this business and see what happens, let's take this trip and see what happens? We're not there. The *see what happens* has been lost, even in small things, like cooking a meal in a new way.

The result is that people are not satisfied, so they move from place to place, they go through friends, they go through occupations, they go through activities, always trying to create something that can't be created, because *vamos a ver que pasa* has been left behind. Life becomes a violation of a basic human regulation as determined by something far greater than us, and we wonder why it's problematic. We wonder why we are never satisfied. We wonder why we're always restless. We wonder why nothing is ever good enough – it always needs a little tweak. We are swimming upstream against that law, and it's not a civil law, it's not a municipal law, it's not a federal law, and it's not even whatever the U.N. laws are called. It's a law that *all* of us are subject to, because this is an experiment.

In the book *Demian*, Herman Hesse describes humans as, "A unique and valuable experiment on the part of nature." People like being described as unique, but . . . experiments? If Hesse had written that human beings are *an experiment on the part of nature,* and left out the *unique*, far fewer people would be enamored of that book. We don't like the idea that we're an experiment; we've gotten very far away from feeling *vamos a ver que pasa.* Not so far away though, that returning to it is out of the question. After all, we do like the moments when we are tricked by circumstance into situations where we have to wait to *see what happens* – and our lives are richer for those moments.

Chapter 41
Escape from Alcatraz

When I go to foreign places I like to rent a car and get lost in the countryside – I mean really get lost. Bulgaria certainly is a place where you can do that – take a few turns onto roads that are barely on the map and see where they lead, or don't lead. It involves a lot of u-turns and asking directions. At some point we were driving through Bulgaria and saw two people driving a wooden horse cart pulled by an old horse, which I learned is not unusual in rural Bulgaria.

In most, if not all countries around the world, the young people gravitate to the cities, and the older people are left in the countryside. Bulgaria is no different, and this couple was probably in their seventies. It was a very sunny, warm day, and to protect their heads from the sun they were wearing paper hats made of newspaper, like you would fold up at a party, like paper crowns.

In the weeks before we left the U.S., we put some energy into learning basic Bulgarian language, and got somewhat familiar with their alphabet – it's called Cyrillic. If you don't know the sounds these letters represent, you can't read signs – especially road signs.

We stopped to ask the couple directions, and when they looked over at us they had big smiles on their faces. They were pointing to their hats, and we didn't know why. One of our theories was that they wanted us to know that they didn't always ride around in paper hats.

I'll tell you why I mentioned these hats, but first I want to tell you about something else that happened on this particular trip. I remembered it when I was doing my laundry this morning. I was going through my pants pockets to make sure they were empty, and found a coin in one of my jeans. It was a British 10 pence coin that I got as change from buying a bottle of water in Heathrow Airport in London, where I had a stopover on my flight back to California from Bulgaria. I tossed it in my catch-all drawer because it has no value to me here in the U.S., other than it reminded me of something I read while I was waiting for my flight.

Heathrow Airport requires a substantial amount of waiting. They are really not set up like we are here in the U.S., or even in Asia, where the airports are really state-of-the-art. People who go through Heathrow have to be more self-sufficient, because most other airports have a fairly decent amount of diversions available, including facilities where you can eat yourself into a stupor. Not so at Heathrow, so we ended up having to entertain ourselves with the couple of guitars that we carried along.

There was also nothing to do at the gate, which is usually the place of duty-free shops and food. Not only was there nothing, but you couldn't even enter the waiting room. We had to wait in the hallway, so we ended up sitting there on the floor for a couple of hours, and that's when I read the magazine article that I want to tell you about.

Recently a man named Frank Morris surfaced in Ireland – you probably don't know that name, I wouldn't have either. Frank Morris, now in his eighties, decided it was time to announce who he was, and that he was still alive. Frank Morris, who now lives in Ireland, used to live in San Francisco – Alcatraz prison more precisely. He was the man played by Clint Eastwood in the movie *Escape from Alcatraz*.

He escaped about 50 years ago. Law enforcement people had guaranteed that no one could ever live through an escape from Alcatraz, and said that he had to have died. In the movie that's what they say in the end, and in the police report that's what they say. Turns out he is alive and well, and has been living in Ireland for the last 40 years or so. Now he is telling the rest of his story, the part that people don't know. People know the part of the story about how he and the two Anglin brothers built dummies of themselves, and put them in their beds with the heads sticking out, so the guards would see them when they walked through. But after that no one knew exactly what happened – they could only guess.

He told the whole story about how they planned it, and how they had someone to get them out of the country. There were different stages of how he ended up in Ireland. He had a distant relative there who arranged some things for him, so he ended up having a life in a rural area of Ireland. The details were in the article, so it was mildly interesting, but of course the most exciting parts were in the movie. The movie depiction of the escape was fairly accurate, because it was known that they crawled through some vent and probably had a blowup raft waiting for them. They also left some of their clothing in the ocean, so people would think they had died, and would stop looking for them.

What Frank Morris didn't know, was what happened to the Anglin brothers after they landed in San Francisco, because they went their separate ways. Frank Morris was the brains of the escape. He knew exactly what to do, but he needed some people to go along with him, and they of course needed him. They needed him completely, because he had the plan and knew the pitfalls along the way. He had worked out all the details.

Morris said in the article, "I've never known where the Anglin brothers went, or what happened with their lives – I'm curious about that." That's interesting, because one might think that they'd be joined at the hip after escaping from Alcatraz together. Maybe they'd go into the dry cleaning business, or whatever people do when they have some intense experience like that together. But they didn't. They got to San Francisco and parted ways, never to see or hear from each other again. Nobody ever caught him, and nobody ever caught the Anglin brothers, so he didn't know what had happened with them, and he wondered.

That's all I can tell you about that story, but I can tell you about the connection between the British coin I found in my pocket, and the relationship between Frank Morris and the Anglin brothers. They were temporarily extremely valuable to each other, extremely important for a time. In order to get water or anything else in the Heathrow airport, I needed something like this coin, but now, in the U.S., it has no value – as Frank Morris no longer has value to the Anglin brothers. They may have needed him absolutely, but it was only for a time.

This example takes me to describing the connection between a spiritual teacher and a spiritual student, and what we can understand about it from this story. If a student is eventually successful in escaping from their prison (the limitations and restrictions of mechanical unconscious life), it would be obvious that they would never have accomplished that escape without following the teacher's expertise – an expertise that they couldn't do without.

How they're going to live their life after they've succeeded in their escape, and what they are going to become as they become themselves, is a story that is really none of a spiritual teacher's business. A teacher may be curious as the years pass, and wonder what ever happened with this or that particular student – that is understandable – but that student is no longer joined at the hip with the teacher. The relationship they had was based on escape, and that is a limited one – an extremely relevant and critical one, but a temporary one.

In order for a student to escape, they need to follow the teacher. They need to watch the teacher closely for instructions, because he or she is the one who knows how to escape, and the student does not. In fact, the teacher is the only one who knows clearly the prison the student is in. A student is not a permanently-affixed follower or creation of the teacher. The student should become a creation of him or herself – a feat of which they are not now capable. All the student is capable of doing now is stamping out license plates. All a student is capable of doing is what mechanical unconscious life allows them to do – like it must have been in Alcatraz. The student's Alcatraz is the infrastructure that they have become a part of – the infrastructure of rules about what's right and wrong, what's good and what's bad, and what's possible and what's not possible.

If you aspire to becoming that student, or imagine that you are already that student, then you must understand that every unexamined concept, and every program that you've become a party to, has established the limitations of your life, the prison of your life. The fact that you have been allowed to decorate your cell in individual ways, is only necessary so that you will be a more obedient prisoner. You may have your little specialties, and your little imaginations about yourself, but all they do is deceive you into believing that your life is flexible – especially we who live in this affluent western world. If the sun is too strong, we don't go outside, or we wear a baseball hat, but we certainly don't fold up paper hats to put on our heads – even for fun. Our restrictive self-image would never allow for that creativity. It would be much too dangerous.

We have the illusion that we have this flexibility; we have our houses, we have our toys, we have our cars, we have our air conditioning, we have all these things. Our cells look pretty darn spiffy, but they are cells nonetheless. Our lives are extremely limited, although when we compare ourselves to other prisoners we feel very fortunate. But we are only comparing ourselves to other prisoners – not to free people, and not to what we ourselves could possibly be.

The Anglin brothers realized that they needed Frank Morris, because it was clear to them that they had life sentences, they all had life sentences. I don't know what the crimes involved were, but they were not satisfied to live that limited prison life, and they were going to take a chance. They were going to take the chance to disrupt their comfort and their sleep, because in prison you are certainly allowed to sleep, even allowed to do nothing sometimes.

If you do what you are told, if you obey the rules, always have your driver's license in your pocket, don't raise your voice in a place where you are not specifically allowed to raise it, then you can get along.

The Anglin brothers were not satisfied just to get along, and Frank Morris was not satisfied either. He knew a way to get out of the prison, and if they went along with it, and a few things broke in their favor (as they need to in ours as well), they might actually escape. They certainly knew how much they needed him in order to escape. Then after they executed this escape and they were in San Francisco, their value to each other was no longer existent, like the value of the 10 pence coin.

So if you come to a place where you are feeling the relevance for a teacher in your life, that feeling should really be very precise. A teacher's function is to help you remember that you are in jail, that you are a prisoner, that your life options are extremely limited, although they appear not to be. That relationship is based on helping you see from moment to moment how distorted your thinking is, how corrupt your decisions are, how far from reality your conclusions are, how you are not the giving person you imagine yourself to be, how you are restricted to being a self-serving person. You are not really living; you are simulating living.

It takes a while to prove that to yourself, to verify that for yourself, but in time you can discover that your imagined acts of goodness are really acts of self-serving and coincidental goodness. Your life is a sequence of feeling bad and recovering from feeling bad, feeling bad and recovering from feeling bad, all the while trying to distort the picture by making up stories that you never really were feeling bad, and didn't need to recover from feeling bad. The tension and stress you feel is not from those external circumstances that you consider unfortunate, but from the dishonest scrambling required to do this self-calming.

As you begin to understand this, and are no longer okay with the extraordinary limitations that you've inadvertently, not deliberately, allowed to be placed on your existence, a teacher who is an expert in this subject, and experienced in this area, can begin helping you plan your escape to freedom, so that you can then go on to become yourself. Concurrent with making these plans, you will need to be reminded of the necessity of escape. Without those reminders, you will be incapable of maintaining the motivation to escape, because the waters of San Francisco Bay are cold and very unpredictable, and your cell is warm and very predictable.

Chapter 42
A Fable on a Foible

A morsel of fiction to cleanse the palate.

There was no way we were going to make it on time. What a ridiculous situation. The four of us sitting on the front steps of my house, luggage all around us, with reservations for a plane due to take off in forty minutes, their car in the shop, ours with a dead battery, and a cab on the way. New York seemed a longer way off from L.A. than it had two months ago, when we planned this trip with our friends. No other available reservations for five days, and oh yes, we live forty minutes from the airport. All is lost.

The cab arrives. None of us have the spirit left to even put the luggage in the cab. We're all sitting on the steps, watching this bouncy little cab driver hustling around, opening the trunk, and putting in our stuff. We all feel sorry for the little guy, not knowing how late we are and all. Our friends go inside to call to see if the plane is taking off on time (it is), and I tell the cabbie the situation.

He listens to me while continuing to put the luggage in the cab, nodding his head as he keeps saying, "No problem, I can get you there." Five times he says this, until our friends decide he's nuts, and take their bags out of the cab. For some crazy lack of a reason, my traveling partner,

Felicity, and I get in the cab, and as it speeds off I roll down the window and call out to my friends, "We'll see you in a little while."

Well, we didn't see them in a little while, but what did happen is that we rode, or should I say floated to the airport. The cabbie talked nonstop the whole way, I think to keep our attention off the unusual movements of the cab, which seemed to hover just enough above the road (great shocks, I thought) to circumvent every obstacle in our path.

I lost all track of time listening to the comments of this fascinating fellow, and the next thing I knew we were driving past the departure terminal. I looked at my watch and we still had fifteen minutes to spare.

It was a little surprising to us that he drove clear over to the hangar area, but we both had confidence that he must know some kind of shortcut. He came to a stop after going through a gate that lead to one of the runways and turned around to us and said, "Here we are."

After seeing how confused we looked, he informed us that from the moment he picked us up, he could tell we were the kind of people that could take advantage of an unusual opportunity. He then proceeded to tell us that an airplane was unnecessary, and that we could remain in the taxi, and it could take us all the way to New York. We of course looked at each other and laughed nervously, and reassured him that we thought his sense of humor was really cute, but under the circumstances we had only a few minutes to make our plane, and that this was no longer the time for jokes. He reiterated his claim of having a flying taxi, told us that all we had to do was relax, and reminded us that having doubts was not a productive habit. This was a lesson that we had both previously learned, and for this reason were more inclined to trust this unusual fellow.

While we were discussing the matter in the back seat of the taxi, our driver, who said we should call him Pal, started making strange noises in his throat (somewhat like the revving of an engine), and then proceeded to drive over to one of the closed runways with grass growing up between the cracks in the concrete. He began to *taxi*, if you will excuse the expression. Naturally, we were in shock, but were at this point irrevocably committed to the insanity, so without being told to do so, we both put on our seat belts.

After reaching what was without a doubt the highest speed I had ever experienced in a car, we came to a gradual stop near the end of the runway. Pal turned around, looked us sincerely in the eyes, and explained with calm and patience, that the only possible reason that we weren't getting off the ground was because we were resisting and not relaxing. He went on to say that he would do all that was necessary to make this flight possible, and all we had to do was sit back and let him do it, and that was, as he put it, "the least we could do in appreciation of his monumental task."

What can be said about our condition at this time? We were no longer functioning by the standards of the "real world." This fellow, Pal, had somehow hijacked our imaginations, and as unbelievable as the whole thing sounded just moments before, we found ourselves turned toward each other, telling one another that we really did have to relax, because resistance never produces any positive results.

Those throat noises again, louder this time, and off we went rolling down the runway, the needle on the speedometer went out of sight, and just as before, we eventually came to a rolling stop at the opposite end of the airport.

Needless to say, another lecture followed, this one striking closer to home, being much more pointed. He was right on every point, and as before, his lecture was followed by a discussion between my partner and me about how we had to do better. It was four o'clock in the afternoon. Our plane had already soared over our heads. We had just completed our 22nd run, and I was disoriented to say the least. Run # 23, same throat noises, but halfway down the runway this time Pal sighed loudly, "Ahhhh." He looked down out of his window and back a little, just like you do when you're in a *you know what*, and said, "We're on our way."

I hadn't opened my eyes on the runway since #17, so it took me a while to absorb what was supposed to be happening. As I finally did open my eyes, what I saw was some strange combination of being in the air and being on the runway – clouds going by on the ground. We definitely weren't flying, but then again, what were those clouds doing on the ground? I was too confused to assess anything, so I just closed my eyes and started feeling sorry for myself for getting into this whole thing, but Felicity was sitting next to me jumping up and down on the seat with excitement. I guess I caught a little from her, because my mood changed drastically, and I got excited too.

At that point I opened my eyes to take a good look, and my good look told me that we had never really left the ground, and that Felicity had lost her marbles, not to speak of the individual in the front seat. I said, "Pal, we're on the ground, we never left the runway." Pal said, "Of course we left the runway, but we had to land again because you stopped trusting me." Guess whose side Felicity was on – but that couldn't be taken into account, because she loved to have support disagreeing with me. I looked around to see if we were at the Los Angeles airport, but runways all look the same. Eventually Pal said it was L.A. airport, and that we had landed there because we hadn't gotten far away when I started to doubt.

How do you think that made me feel? Well, just as I began to get into just how that made me feel, the throat noises started, and we were doing it again. I had almost no resistance left, so for quite some time, maybe hours, days, weeks, months, years, what difference does it make, my whole world became a series of take-offs, landings, taxiings, discussions about trust, relaxing, resisting, moments of elation, depression, being sure I was in the air, on the ground, out of my mind. The funny thing was, that although I know that I never got to New York, I was never quite sure whether or not our interim landings (caused by either my doubt or my partner's) were not actually at some airport closer to New York.

Well now you have the background, and that takes us up to what happened this morning. We were taxiing for the umpteenth time, and all of a sudden I heard the words shout out of my mouth, "I'VE HAD ENOUGH!" The cab rolled to a stop and I said the following: "Okay look, this has been an incredible experience. There's no one who could say this hasn't been an incredible experience. Sometimes I really believe that your cab really can fly, and other times it looks like an ordinary cab to me. Sometimes I think it's my doubt that keeps us on this runway, and other times I think that you don't know what the hell you're doing. You know what?

Sometimes I even think the cab can fly, it's just that you're not that good a pilot. But usually I'm just depressed, because maybe I'm keeping this whole trip from getting off the ground.

"So what's the difference? Maybe it's me, maybe it's you, maybe it's the cab, maybe it's the weather, I mean – what's the difference? I'm still not in New York. I'd ask you to drop me off at the passenger terminal, but at this point I'm not sure that even an airplane would get me there. I guess all I'm sure of, is I have to try something else. I remember when you first picked us up to drive us to the airport. . . it was exciting. . . no doubt about it."

Now there was nothing left to say, so I got out of the cab and heard the door close behind me. I'm not sure what Felicity did, because I didn't want to turn around. Pal could be very convincing. He probably could have talked me into one more try. I think that's what happened to her.

The End

I have included this story for a very specific reason. It's an example of a spiritual tool that can be too easily misinterpreted, thus making it inefficient and potentially harmful. When I wrote this story many years ago, it was extremely meaningful to me. In rereading it now it still is, but after having numerous spiritual seekers read it, I have yet to find more than one or two who grasp my meaning.

Whether we are aware of it or not, we have been programmed to expect stories, whether they be in movies, or in books, to have certain reliable structures. There is a hero. There is a victim. There are supporting characters. There is a thread of consistency and reason that guides the story. In a spiritual or metaphysical or esoteric story, a person who exhibits a power for good is automatically a hero who can do no wrong. Similarly, a person that fails to benefit from exposure to that hero is weak and defective, and those traits are indefensible.

Pal may have incredible abilities, as do many spiritual teachers – but if one of those abilities doesn't include realizing when an aspirant is not able to absorb their teaching, and suggesting they try elsewhere – then that teacher, not the aspirant, is negligent. Tools and methods are only relevant if, with sincere application, they support a person's pursuit. If those tools or methods require a superhuman effort, then they are not what they are put forth to be, because aspirants are at best human, and never superhuman.

Yes, Pal's passengers were not ready to take advantage of his remarkable capacity, but the responsibility for that deficiency is still his, not theirs. They made a considerable sustained effort, and proved to be incapable of benefiting from his manifestations. Were Pal to take responsibility, he would have to either present his aspirants with new methods, or advise them that their efforts would better be placed elsewhere.

Teachers of any subject are not all of the same caliber, and often are only a step or two ahead of their students. This doesn't mean that someone can't learn from another who is far from perfect. Similarly, spiritual teachers, regardless of what exotic land they are from, may only be a step or two ahead of their students. They may not be of a state of being to exhibit the level of responsibility required to suggest a person try elsewhere.

The spiritual group dynamic is a complex one. At one moment it can be dramatically supportive, and the next mutually self-destructive. It is the responsibility of the person in charge of that group, to protect students from the latter to the best of his or her ability. The tendency of people in a support group, is to want others that are attracted to that group to remain faithful, no matter what. It is not only the Pal of the group who must be aware of this tendency, but his or her elder students as well. Their enthusiasm should not be thoughtlessly unleashed. Not that they have the responsibility to encourage people to go elsewhere, but they certainly have the responsibility to avoid convincing people to stay, when they are ready to go.

Assistance from any source, no matter how enlightened it may be, can only be catalytic in nature. The energy that creates and maintains life is received by each individual human being. It is accurate that we humans have a history of obscuring that reception, and without help, re-discovery is all but impossible, but that help must be both solicited and valued. When that valuation terminates, help must be sought elsewhere, but that final decision should always be made by the receiver. If there is value to be extracted from the lines of this story, it is that each individual, with help, must assess where he or she belongs.

Chapter 43

William from Malawi

The first requirement, and by far the most important for anyone who is going to be able to help you spiritually, is that person has to be able to do two things – mail a letter, and pass the salt. If a person can't mail a letter for you, and pass the salt to you, then you can rule them out. That rules out a lot of people. That eliminates all the people who are no longer alive – all of them. Not a single one of them can help you, not one of them, because they can't pass the salt to you, and they can't mail a letter for you.

You don't have to consider them anymore. Look at how much I've lightened your load. Every single person from any country, and any culture, with any wisdom, and any accomplishment, no matter how admirable, extraordinary, or enlightened they were – they can't help you because they don't meet the first requirement.

That means that any one of your friends, even if they understand only a little, are not very accomplished, are certainly not enlightened, but can pass the salt to you, and can mail a letter for you, would be on your list before Buddha, Jesus, Rama, Krishna, Yogananda, and Gurdjieff, and everyone else who is no longer alive.

Now we come to the second requirement for someone who can help you spiritually. That person has to be in proximity to you, so as to be able to *actually* pass the salt to you. So they can't only be willing to pass the salt to you – they have to be in a position where they actually can pass the salt to you. So your friends are still in the running, because they can do that.

Not only have we eliminated all the people that are no longer alive, now we're also eliminating all the people who are alive, but aren't close enough to you so you can say, "Would you pass the salt?" That really shrinks down the field, because that includes all the gurus and teachers with large followings. They're certainly not going to be available to pass the salt to you. You couldn't even walk into their house without security getting in your way. You could see them on a stage every once in a while – maybe every year or every six months, or you might be able to see them along with a crowd of people – but salt passing and letter mailing? I don't think so.

To further explore this question of finding a teacher, I want to tell you about William Kamkwamba from Malawi, who is now about eighteen years old. Malawi is an extremely poor agricultural country, where many people live in huts of different kinds, with very rudimentary technology. William lived in a hut with his family with no electricity and a questionable water source, in a village of about twenty families. His village was like one you might read about in National Geographic magazine.

Even though English is their official language, because it was at one time Nyasaland, part of British Central Africa, many people in Malawi speak Chichewa. William spoke English fluently and read a good deal. He went to school when he could, but mostly worked with his family, and read a lot. He was thought of in his village as a nice boy, a bright boy, a helpful boy, and he took care of his family.

At some point, the village elders got together and decided they needed to do something about getting electricity, because other places in the area had gotten electricity. They wanted to start improving their water source, and doing different things that only electricity could facilitate. So they got in touch with some agencies, found out how electricity is established, and how much money would have to be raised to make that happen. They had a community meeting, and everybody was there including William. He was considered an adult because he took care of a lot of things for his family. He wasn't a child any more.

The elders presented the idea of getting electricity, and mentioned the different agencies and professionals that would have to be involved. They made it clear that this would cost a lot of money, and would take a long time, so the project wouldn't be completed for many months – maybe even years.

William stood up at the meeting and said, "I think I could bring electricity to this village. I think I can do that." When this sixteen-year-old, who didn't have any experience doing anything like that, and was mainly known for milking cows and reading a lot, made this claim, people looked at him with kindly smiles, and suggested maybe he could help out when the professionals came.

William repeated, "No, I think I can do this. I can bring electricity to this village. I have some ideas. I have thought about it and read about it, and I think I can do it."

No one took William seriously, so the village borrowed money and hired a solar consultant to write a report and make a plan for them. Six months later nothing much had happened – the consultant had just gotten started writing his report, but he did send a few bills.

By this time William had become even more confident. He said, "Before, I thought I could do it, but now I know I can do it, so please let me try." Since they had nothing to lose, they placated him by asking what materials he would need. He told them that he didn't need anything from the outside, nor did he need any money. Of course this evoked even less confidence from the elders, who didn't have much in the first place.

William did it. He built a windmill out of local materials, and then he built a second one, and created an electrical system for the town. A sixteen-year-old kid who milked cows and read a lot did it. The story of what happened in William's village went out on the web, and now he has started his own company. He's eighteen now.

The reason I'm bringing up this story is not because it is a successful third world electricity development story. It's a nice story in itself, but that's not why I'm bringing it up. The people in his village had a concept. It went something like: *How can he do it? I couldn't do it, and he's just like me. He looks like me, he grew up where I grew up, he knows the people that I know, he eats the food I eat, he milks the cows I milk. He does the things I do; how could he do anything that I couldn't do?*

But they were wrong, because he could. I'm giving you some guidelines about where to look, and what not to overlook. Because when you are looking for people who are no longer alive, and you are looking for people who are from other cultures who look different, and speak differently, and wear different clothes, and have a different ethnicity than you, you may have overlooked the William amongst you. So if somebody amongst you claims that they can help you, and you dismiss that person, you may be dismissing that person because they look like you, they talk like you, they come from where you come from, they eat the food that you eat, and they wear the clothes that you wear.

So, I've given you three guidelines so far: the salt, the mail, and proximity. They have to be available to you, and they may be closer to you than you think.

Chapter 44

Currency of Struggle

Most of our circumstances are, at worst, relatively pleasant. Most of our conflicts are self-generated, and even when they are externally produced, they are generally mild. We live in a part of the world that is basically strife free, for not all, but for a majority of the population. There are no armed insurrections going on, minimal chaos – things are pretty orderly for most of us. All in all, it sounds like a pretty soft deal for most people in the western world. It's an acceptable situation, tolerable most of the time, and frequently pretty sweet.

How is it that some people get mildness, mellowness and circumstances of natural beauty, and others have conditions that are so extraordinarily different, that life for them is a struggle for food, clothing, and shelter, and sometimes even for safety? How is it that some people get life as a struggle, and others get life not as a struggle?

I know this question gives you trouble – I know that it

does. What we call *making a living* is really a gross and disgusting term for us, because we don't really have to *make* a living. Our culture *gives* us a living. There are people who actually do have to make a living; we don't make a living – we take advantage of the living we're given. If you have never had to miss a meal – if you have the leisure to read and talk about extraordinary things – if you have time to explore and experiment, while millions of people have to make sure they have food, clothing, and shelter, then you are troubled by that question.

How could it be so inequitable, that some people actually have to make their way so that they can survive, and other people get all that, plus leisure granted to them, as you and I do? You and I have room for something called a spiritual quest – a quest for internal freedom. How much leisure is that? Leisure to the extreme. Unless you totally isolate your life, and choose not to notice people in foreign countries, or even this country, who have to struggle for necessities, that conflict must give you trouble.

I'm going to try to explain something that may help you embark on and maintain a spiritual quest, without having to contend with, and be challenged by that conflict. Rather than be inhibited by it, you could be inspired by it, be enthused by it, be motivated by the absurdly-appearing dichotomy between the people who have so much, as we do, and the many millions who have so little. What is the point of a creation, an experiment, with such extreme circumstances of life?

In actuality, though circumstances may be diverse, there is a common denominator for all human beings. What we have all been given is a stage for struggle, and the players are either struggling, or they aren't on that stage. They are, you might even say, filler, fodder for the people who are on that stage.

I'm going to explain what I mean by this word, struggle. It is the commodity, or more like the *currency* of participation in human life, and everyone has an equal chance to participate. It's clear that *our* potential struggles are very different than *their* potential struggles. They are struggling for food, clothing, shelter, and security. What are *we* struggling for that makes us equals, and not separate from them? If those of us who have been granted the benefits of the affluent world have taken up the next challenge, then we are not *more* privileged than they, and we are not *less* privileged than they. We are all players on the same stage if we recognize what *we* have to struggle with, and are fully engaged in that struggle.

The normal inclination of a comfortable person is to feel that there's something missing, that there is a deficiency in their life that demands a new goal. Since people don't know that there is a next goal, different from the last one, they proceed to struggle with what other people are struggling with, except that they have already done that, so they have to struggle for more and more.

We have the opportunity to recognize that we have enough and even excess. It can begin to occur to us, that the repetition of that cycle of getting a little bit more, a little bit more, a little bit easier, a little bit more leisure, a little more this, a little more that, is indulgent and empty. There are those of us to whom it has occurred that getting more might not be the path to anything of substance or depth of meaning. Those of us who have paid attention, recognize that *a little bit more* carries something with it that actually makes it a little bit less. So we start to yearn for escape from that cycle, and start to look for something else. That is when the opportunity to play on that stage opens up to us in a very unique and interesting way – a new kind of struggle.

The struggle for money, for attention, for recognition, for comfort – even the struggle for control is no longer your struggle. That's over. Of course you have to maintain the basics, but the idea that these are your struggles is over. You've found a way to feed yourself, to clothe yourself, to shelter yourself and a lot more – and it's sufficient. You may get a little more, you may get a little less, but engaging in that struggle is no longer relevant for you, if you are to be on the stage of life, and not just filler or fodder.

Your natural inclination to struggle is now meant to be put in another arena – the arena of struggling toward consciousness, toward awareness. Now, your struggle is with your lack of attention, with your lack of concentration, struggle with your inability to get beneath the surface of things, struggle with your negative opinions of other people, struggle with your blame and self-pity, and all the other obstacles that are in between you and the beautiful experience of being a servant – not for your own pleasure, but because the world desperately needs people who have those qualities.

You no longer have to struggle for food, clothing, and shelter to keep busy. There is so much to be occupied with that is appropriate for *your* struggle. Yes, you will have to work, you will have to either hammer nails or fill out papers or punch keys on the computer. You will do that. You will spend your time in those ways. But it won't be your struggle, it won't be your quest, it won't be your challenge.

You will start to feel differently about yourself in relation to the poor and the down-trodden, and all the other people in this world who have very difficult external circumstances, including threats to their physical safety. You may even find yourself assisting those people in some way, but not from your guilt, not from discomfort with your own good fortune.

In a curious way, those who struggle for the essentials may have a more straightforward task than those of us who are struggling toward consciousness. First of all, we are dealing with an elective choice, because external circumstances don't demand our struggle. We have the option to stay off the stage of life, even though it might bring us numbness, and cost us our humanity. Secondly, we have two obligations, as opposed to the one obligation of survival held by those in poverty or in harm's way. We must not only work as hard as they do at *our* endeavor, but we must lend assistance, in any way we can, to those who are actually trying to make a living – or more precisely, trying to keep themselves and their families living.

If you are actually struggling for consciousness, your life will not be easy. It will be difficult, but in a different way from those who lack the essentials. Perhaps we should use another term than *struggle* to define our work, because it's not strain, and it's not suffering. It's going against. Going against self-destructive tendencies can take tremendous effort, as can going against the momentum of numbness and blame, and all the different forms of negativity and darkness. Similarly, it can take a tremendous effort to go against our laziness, our mechanical ways of acting, our false confidence, and our tendency to blindly accept what we've been taught.

There are so many opportunities to struggle, that if you really were fully involved in what people have historically called *the work,* not *the play*, you would not, at the end of the day, feel so separate from those who have been given other assignments of struggle. You would not feel elite, or separate, or different. You would feel that they have their struggle, and you have yours. But you would not feel guilty, because there is no guilt if you are working hard, and they are working hard. Understand, those of you who have been given the gift of leisure, have been given it so that you can struggle with your lack of consciousness. If you do, your confusion will be replaced by an overwhelming sense of belonging to the un-exclusive experiment called the human race.

Certainly you can refute what you've been reading, and your heart will still continue to beat. The power that creates breath and heartbeat doesn't enforce the requirement to struggle, but you will not be having the experience of a natural human being. You will be a passer of time, and a passer of time is far, far short of what a human being can be. Human beings are those who struggle for food, clothing, and shelter, along with their brothers and sisters who are struggling for consciousness. The only way you can really verify the equitability of those struggles is to engage in them. When you do, you'll feel a unique connection to history and time, because you will be a player on the stage of life. You will be paying with the currency of struggle.

Chapter 45
Building the Voyager

As I mentioned in the previous chapter, those of us who wish to be fully human have two obligations – one is to struggle with our obstacles to consciousness, and the other, to help those who are lacking in the basics. Some friends and I were attempting to fulfill that second obligation in Turkey on the Syrian border last November. We were there to do some social work activity in relation to the Syrian refugees. We spent a month doing what we could both for our own benefit, and for their benefit, till eventually it was time to come home. Over my years of traveling, I have discovered different ways of making the trip home from either Europe, or the Middle East. Of course there is flying in one shot, sometimes with a short stopover, then there is stopping over for a few days in some interesting place in the middle.

Some years ago I discovered a third option – traveling on a repositioning cruise ship. These are large fancy ships that go around the Mediterranean in the summer, then go around the Caribbean in the winter. Of course in between, they have to sail from one ocean to the other, and that's what they call repositioning. Ordinarily it would be very expensive to spend two weeks on a cruise ship (the time it takes to cross the Atlantic), but since they have to make that trip anyway, the cost becomes reasonable – actually less than plane fare. If you have the time, and if spending two weeks on the ocean is attractive to you, then a ship can be an option. So that's how I got home from Europe a few months ago.

If you haven't been on a cruise boat before, and maybe even have the attitude that I originally had – that cruises are for the newlyweds and the nearly deads, the ship option would definitely sound unattractive. Cruise ships are like whole cities of 3,000 people – 2,000 who are called passengers, and about 1,000 people who are working to keep those passengers happy. Although these boats are huge, it's still 3,000 people living in this fairly limited space.

Everything needed to care for these people for two weeks has to be on board, because if it's not on the boat, it's not getting on the boat. That means all the food, the entertainment, the safety stuff, the fuel and everything else needed for the running of the boat.

In each of the 1,000 rooms, called cabins, which are actually well-equipped hotel rooms, there's a TV that shows the usual satellite programs, in addition to some documentary programs about the cruise line itself. One of the documentaries that I saw while sailing across the Atlantic Ocean at twenty knots was called *The Making of the Voyager*. The Voyager is the name of one of the largest cruise boats at 140,000 tons, and a quarter of a mile long. This documentary described in detail what had to be done to build and equip a boat much larger than any ever built before.

One of the scenes in this documentary was of a round table conference of all the people who were in charge of the different areas that needed to be covered. To mention only a few, there was the chief engineer, who dealt with the engines and motorized equipment, the hotel room designer, the food service manager, who supervises the running of a dozen different restaurants, the architects and structural experts that design the entire ship, and of course the captain, who will eventually command the boat and be in overall charge when at sea.

Everyone around this very large round table had their unique area of interest that they wanted considered in building the Voyager. From what we know about human nature, for each of them, their area was the most important part of the process, because they were responsible for it getting accomplished. Obviously, if somebody is in charge of the entertainment and shows on the ship, that's what they're thinking about – that's where they want the most money allocated. They want the most space allocated to their specialty, and they want the fanciest state-of-the-art equipment available. That's understandable. The film was covering this discussion in which everybody obviously couldn’t get what they want, or the ship would be as big as a city and cost as much to build.

So someone has to have an overview in order to set the priorities and make the necessary decisions. Someone has to have an overview of how this all fits together. Eventually the captain will be the commander of the ship, but he’s a sailor, not a hotel operator, not a show producer, not a restaurant manager – he can’t be the person with an overview. They were having difficulty finding someone without a vested interest in some element. The most challenging part of this process appeared to be getting the people involved to subordinate to some overriding principle represented by someone – someone who has the authority to say, "We can't have the gym take up this whole floor, because then we'll have no room for the casino, and we'll have no room for the buffet."

I found it really fascinating, because each person was a very talented and very knowledgeable expert in his or her field. Then there was the architect who had to make it all work structurally. So, when the theater person said that she didn't want any posts to block people's view in the theater – the architect, remembering that he's building a boat and not a building, had to decide if it's possible. He knows that you can't sink supports into the ocean, and everything is resting on something. We're watching the architect having somewhat of a nervous breakdown, because he's trying to make it all happen, and he can't make everyone happy.

The first forty-five minutes of this hour-and-a-half documentary takes place in this room where these people are sincerely trying to work together, because they all want this great boat to happen, and it's just not happening. It's not happening until they discover the need for someone to represent an overriding principle for this process – someone to have the say of what is realistic to happen here by looking at, not this segment or that segment, but the whole thing.

Eventually the president of the corporation decided to bring in a Hollywood film producer who knows nothing about ships, but has overseen major productions. This man's only credential was that he had been successfully supervising multi-faceted, multi-million dollar operations where everything depends on something else.

The idea, is that this person is going to absorb the expertise of everyone else, and though he would have no particular shipboard knowledge, he would be able to ask the right questions.

The similarity between their predicament and their need for representation of an overriding principle, is not far away from our human condition. Those of us who live our lives in western culture are not aware of that necessity. We're not aware that within ourselves there are interest groups. We may not be *part* of a production of different interest groups – we *are* a production of different interest groups.

We have parts of us that want to go off on our own, and parts of us that want to raise a family, and parts of us that want to start our own business, and parts of us that don't want to have the responsibility of a business, and parts of us that want to live in the city where there is activity all the time, and parts of us that can't stand activity and want to be out in the country. We have parts of us that like being around people, and parts of us that can't stand being around people.

We have a production going on within us, and we have no overriding principle, so we're constantly under the influence of the part of us that happens to have the loudest voice in the moment. And if the loudest voice is the food voice, the restaurant voice, the gym voice, the theater voice, the engine room voice, then *that* idea will get the attention. That attention can lead to a decision that does not serve the whole, which can in fact be destructive to the whole, even though it appears to be a good idea in the moment – at least for the part of our corporation that is speaking loudest.

Unfortunately, when that whole corporation gets together, when that whole production gets together, it doesn't seem to work, and we don't know why. So we try to solve each problem individually. Our life becomes a process of solving our problems, our plans, and our relationships. We have very little time for anything else. We're always in the midst of solving something, and our picture of how that takes place is by taking each individual thing – our money issue . . . okay, solve it. Our relationship issue . . . okay solve that, our housing issue . . . solve that. Our health issue . . . solve that – and so on, and so on, and so on, not recognizing that we do not have an overriding principle.

I've sailed from the U.S. to Europe on that Voyager ship. It's outrageous. That ship actually did get built, but only after they recognized what was needed for all these self-interest groups to be able to operate together. We need to understand that situation in our lives, but we are not in optimal conditions for learning the lesson that we are deficient in that overriding principle. Even if we have the concept that we're not deficient, because we're spiritual seekers, or free spirits, or business persons, or family persons, or whatever concept we have of ourselves, that concept does not rule, when it comes to all the different interest groups that arise in us. You are not one thing, and you have no overriding principle.

It does take certain conditions to learn this very important lesson. You will not learn it in ordinary life, because ordinary life is set up to defend the concept of problems, plans, and relationships and their individual solutions. The people that you know, and the people that you seek out for counsel, whether it's your parents or your friends – whether it's in person or in books, have not had the realization that an overriding principle is necessary.

They will more likely either ignore you, wait until you're finished complaining so they can complain, or they will try to give you their formula for the solution of your particular problem of the moment – the money problem, the relationship problem, the housing problem, the job problem, the health problem. But they will not be able to contribute an overriding principle, because its necessity is not their reality.

In the case of building the Voyager ship, the absence of an overriding principle eventually became clear. All the interest groups at least had a common denominator – they wanted to make a beautiful ship that people would love sailing on, where they would spend their money and return again and again. They all wanted that. Once they got someone to represent the importance of an overriding principle that was greater than the sum of its parts, they were able to build the ship. They didn't have to make one up. They just had to be reminded to adhere to it.

Our situation is the same. We don't have to create one. We don't have to fabricate one. We have to rediscover the overriding principle that's always been there. In order to subordinate all these individual interest groups in us to that principle, we have to rediscover it so tangibly, that it becomes our reality. If it's only our philosophy, our rap, our jargon, no subordination will happen – only chaos. That overriding principle has to be realized in ourselves, re-discovered in ourselves. It is something that we were born with, something that is the birthright of a human being. We have lost the recognition of the tangible reality that was once our guiding principle, and our only hope for peace is in finding it again.

Chapter 46
The Lifeguard

Some years ago, I was in Thailand doing social work with a group of people. When our project was completed, some of us took some time to travel around to different places, and one of the places we went to was Malaysia. We ended up going to a sleepy little island called Lankawii. It was a beautiful island that the government was planning to turn into an international resort. In order to do that, they signed a contract with Sheraton Hotels to build a super exclusive resort on the island. Of course, we didn't know that at the time. We thought we were going to a picturesque little island with cheap shacks lining the beach, such as is popular in Asia.

When we arrived at the boat dock on this island, a lady in a business suit came up to us and said, “Would you like to go to the Sheraton resort?” We told her we had nothing like that in mind, but she explained that we wouldn’t have to pay for anything. Evidently, they had just opened the resort, and were looking for Westerners to find out about the place, so we were being asked to stay for free. That wasn’t a difficult decision to make, so we went.

The place was truly outrageous. They gave us a chalet that was all of solid teak. It was magnificent – swimming pools, tennis courts, everything. They even had brand new windsurfing equipment with all the latest gear. As luck would have it, I had been windsurfing for a couple of years, and was capable of doing pretty well if the conditions were okay. The people in charge of the equipment didn’t even know how to put it together, so they were thrilled to have us show them how it worked. We went out in the water and did a little showing off, and a little instructing.

Later that day, I was standing on the balcony of our chalet watching a guy pick up a windsurfing rig and head out into the water. The way he was handling the sail, it was clear that he didn’t know how to windsurf. Something you learn early about windsurfing is that if you don’t sail with the tide, the swell will take you down wind, and you won’t end up where you started. You could end up anywhere, and in this case, the wind was taking this guy out to sea.

I was looking out from my balcony, and I saw this man heading out to sea. I knew what was going to happen because I know windsurfing, and I knew the guys who gave him the equipment don’t. So I went down to where the equipment was, and told the guys who have a boat, that this man was in bad shape. They tell me, "He's okay, he's a strong swimmer." I tried, but I couldn't convey to them that there was a problem.

As it was, the bay had a mouth to it, and as this man was drifting out to sea, he managed to get hooked by the edge of the land. I was looking through my binoculars and could see that he was exhausted. He barely managed to get to the land. He was a mile away from the hotel beach, but at least he was safe. As I was sitting there watching him, he jumped in the water and started to swim back, leaving his board behind. I also see that there are swells in the ocean, and I reasoned that this guy was not going to be able to swim a mile back. He's just not going to be able to do it. So I ran down to the beach again, and showed the guys there that he was trying to swim back without his board.

At this point, even they can see that the situation was bad. When you're in the ocean, the only thing you have going for you is your board. After I showed the guys on the beach the situation, they quickly got their boat ready and set out. I went back to my chalet and saw, through my binoculars, that they picked him up.

I never saw him again, but I know he made it back. I don't know if he ever knew that somebody saved his life, but that's basically what happened. I saw that his life was in jeopardy, and I acted accordingly. It was a bit of a challenge to go up to these guys on the beach a second time, since I had already approached them the first time to warn them, and they told me not to worry. The thoughts in my head said, "Why are you pestering these guys? They probably know what they're doing." But I went down anyway, and this man ended up having his life saved.

The reason I'm telling you this story is because we have a parallel situation going on here. We are dealing with two very tangible realities. One reality is that thousands of people on the planet are starving, dying from diseases that are easily preventable, victims of natural disasters and man-made disasters. It's easy for us to recognize that need. Some people even respond generously to it. Many people give to charity; a lot of people make efforts to help those less materially fortunate than themselves.

We are in the curious position of possibly recognizing another need, a quest other than the one for physical well-being and survival – the quest for spiritual survival. We recognize that need. We are the people who recognize the possibility of spiritual decay or dying. We've been given binoculars, which are our eyes, and we're being asked to volunteer to be the lifeguard – to sit on the balcony and watch our peers, and if anybody appears to be in jeopardy, we could run down, jump in, and save that person.

I'm not talking about having to save your peers at your own peril. I was never in danger of any kind while watching that windsurfer from my balcony. Sure, there was inconvenience, maybe even a little bit of embarrassment. It may even seem like a small thing, but how many of you would go on a list to help someone who has fallen in a spiritual hole? Are you willing to put yourself on that list? "I'll be their lifeguard; I'm responsible, I won't ignore the danger, I'll respond if they need me."

The ordinary interpretation of the word *ignorance,* is not to know something. But there is another meaning for that word; ignorance is ignoring. It's knowing something and choosing not to see it – choosing to say that something is not worthwhile enough to respond to – choosing to see it as too small or unimportant to be inconvenienced by. In a western movie, a cowboy will say, "I'll cover you," that means someone is watching to see that you're not getting into trouble. That's known as, *I've got your back*. That's the opposite of ignoring.

When one of your friends does something questionable, you could ask yourself, "Does she need a mother or father right now? Does he need a lifeguard? Does she need someone to set her straight, someone to lift her out of the trench or the groove she's in? Does he need someone to ask him, *what's going on*?"

If a kid is creating some trouble, someone will ask, "Whose kid is this?" In our situation, in any moment, any one of you could be that kid. You could be the one straying from what is good for you. You could be the one doing something self-destructive. The person observing that self-destructive behavior can immediately become the parent. But since you don't see your friends as your kids, you don't say anything.

Ignoring is self-destructive behavior. You have to allow yourself to pay attention to others, so that you are asking yourself the question, "Is this person in need of a mother or a father right now?" Not a mother or father who has opinions, but one who is concerned. A kid does something, and the parent thinks, "Is it good for them? Will they come out stronger on the other side?" They don't know. Is it good, is it bad? They don't know for sure. As their parent, are they concerned? Yes.

Think of the simple circumstances that have been given to us to practice caring for each other. We don't need to create it. We don't have to travel to far-away places to get that. We don't have to learn exotic methods that existed in times past. We don't need them in order to learn to have concern. No one is in the position of always being the child. No one is always in the position of needing to be rescued from the water. You may have established that position for yourself to avoid responsibility, but always taking that position is a distortion. Sometimes you're the child, and sometimes the parent. You are not helping yourself with that ignoring. Anytime you think, "I can't help because I don't know what is the right thing to do," that is never a bona-fide excuse, because if you had a child, not knowing what to do would not stop you from being concerned.

Having concern for each other will tie us together in a way that we are not tied together now. If you have someone's kid or pet to take care of for a few days, someone you feel responsible for, you have a certain attitude toward that kid or pet. Think of that attitude. Feel that attitude.

That attitude is not one that we have adopted toward each other. By having concern, the possibilities are huge for us to learn how we are not separate. How are you going to learn that? Are you going to learn that from seeing auras? I don't think so. If you ever really learn to see auras, it won't be because you learned a technique. It will be because the separation between you and other people has dissolved to such a degree that you are they, and they are you.

Having concern for others does not mean you have to take on another's burden. There are moments when someone is in front of you. You may not even know their name, but they're in front of you. If they fall down and are lying there, you don't think, "I can't take on another person." If they're in front of you, all you have to do is be there with them in that moment. If you see something is off, and you are there with them in that moment, that person is your child.

If someone is falling down, in any of the ways a person can fall, and you don't feel concern, you're missing the fact that the Creator has put a face and a body in front of you. Your concern will help you to learn all the magical things that can be learned about that person. There are things that you cannot learn any other way.

We've been given each other as a gift. You're not going to invent something better than that. No supernatural phenomenon is going to replace our basic opportunity to look out for each other. When the gazelles go to the water hole, they take turns watching for predators, so they can warn each other if there is trouble. We don't warn each other.

You think that you're getting away with something, but you're not. I say this, because having concern by being a lifeguard for each other is not an *extra* on the spiritual path, it's a basic learning principle on that path.

As a human being on this Earth, your position in this life is very similar to what mine was sitting on that balcony. It's not okay to watch someone floundering and think, "They'll be okay, they can swim, the winds will change," or some such thing. The reason you make those assessments is because you don't want to make the effort to respond. You have your own problems to think about – there's some commitment or embarrassment or inconvenience involved. You think, "Someone else will take care of them," and that's not okay. If you see someone tripping and falling physically, mentally, emotionally, or spiritually, and you're witnessing it, then there *is* no one else. That's why you're there. *You* are their lifeguard.

Justin & Jack

Chapter 47

Credentials

It's a pity we can no longer depend on our intuition and our observations to assess the value and depth of the people whose paths we cross, but we either won't or can't. We live in a world of credentials. Maybe someday we won't – but for now we do – so here are mine.

In the latter part of the fourteenth century, Bahauddin Naqshband, a descendent in the lineage of the Khwajagan Masters of Central Asia, was approached by a young man from eastern Afghanistan who had traveled to Bukhara to become his student. This man, Yaqub al Charkhi, who had already studied for some years under the renowned Egyptian Shaykh as-Shirwani, eventually became the leader of the Naqshbandi Sufis. Along with his duties as the central figure of that order and its many schools, Yaqub, later in life, established an experimental school in the remote northeastern corner of Afghanistan near the village of Shahr-e Monjan in the foothills of the Hindu Kush range. For over 500 years, this school perpetuated the essential creed of the Naqshbandi Sufi tradition, *In this world but not of this world*, though there was often distinct deviation from accepted conventional form. Sufi schools of that time were strictly Islamic, and most followed the orthodoxy of Muslim practice. This was not the case for the unique experiment that Yaqub established. Students and teachers from various faiths and cultures participated – new methods were developed, and old methods modified, according to the needs of those assembled.

Five hundred years after the death of Yaqub, the school that he had established still operated as a place where people, who had been prepared by selected teachers in countries throughout the world, would come to further advance their internal and external spiritual practices, in hopes of attaining intimacy with the ultimate reality, in order to become true servants.

Sometime around 1920 there was in residence at Shahr-e Monjan a small group of students, two of whom showed exceptional promise. These two, Raoul Rainti, the son of an Indian diplomat stationed in Bolivia, and Georgi Ivanovich, a Russian from the Caucasus, were sent by the Shaykh of the school on an expedition to India, to learn meditation from a Sikh Master named Sawan Singh. While in India, they were incorporated into a group of students ranging in age from Georgi Ivanovich, who was the oldest at forty years old, to a much younger man named Hans Ji Maharaj. The other members of the group were Charan Singh, Kirpal

Singh, and Raoul Rainti. These five were taught an ancient form of meditation designed to lead a practitioner, in the most direct way possible, to the experience of the pure and perfect energy of the Creator – not only for their personal self-realization, but for the specific purpose of having them develop as agents who would work toward eventually spreading this knowledge throughout the world.

Raoul Rainti, later known in the Andes mountains of South America as Raya because of his skill at weaving the knotted rugs of the same name, and Georgi Ivanovich, later to become internationally known as G.I. Gurdjieff, maintained contact throughout their lifetimes, and met sporadically over the years. One of those occasions of meeting took place in New York, toward the end of Gurdjieff's life. On that occasion, Gurdjieff invited Raya, who by then was the director of a school in South America, to a party to which he was also invited. The gathering was at a restaurant owned by a family of Russian immigrants, whose son-in-law Yaqub, was a participant in one of Gurdjieff's study groups, and in fact, was named after the founder of the school in Shahr-e Monjan, Afghanistan.

As a special treat at this well-attended party, Yaqub (Americanized Jack) introduced his young son Dusty, who would supply entertainment for the evening by playing a piece on the violin. In the weeks that followed, Raya, after being introduced by Gurdjieff, befriended the family, and took a special liking to little Dusty and vice-versa. On his departure for South America, Raya left an open invitation for Dusty to visit him on the shores of Lake Titicacca on the Peru-Bolivia border.

Some years later, I, no longer called Dusty but Justin – my actual name, made the first of my numerous trips to South America, and became a student of Raya's at his school in Bolivia. After several years of preparation, I was eventually instructed in the meditation that Raya learned from Sawan Singh. When I reached my early twenties, Raya suggested that I participate in group work in the U.S., and recommended a contact in the Gurdjieff Foundation. I became a participant in a group, and studied the methods put forth by this organization that was, and is dedicated to preserving the legacy of G.I. Gurdjieff in the exact manner in which it was presented. This was a curious undertaking for the organization, because Gurdjieff himself often stated that one of the most essential elements of method, were time and place – both of which had drastically changed. I recognized this curiosity, and though it caused some friction for my personality, it didn't dissuade me from trying to learn what they had to teach.

I supplemented this work with independent exploration into the effect of group dynamics, drugs, music, and contact with other seekers, as well as undertaking extensive reading, the latter being an activity that I had never previously pursued. My intermittent contact with Raya remained my most dynamic, and through it, I absorbed an expanding value for the quality of *presence*, in addition to an understanding of numerous revolutionary points of view. Raya maintained that efficient methods for westerners of affluent cultures had yet to be developed, and that his own methods were only occasionally applicable.

Thus he focused his teachings to me, not so much on methods, but on conveying an understanding of, and valuation for, such principals as self-observation, the necessity of heartfelt experience, the nature of obstacles, the destructiveness of mechanical behavior, and the need for an exact language for communication of the components of the precise science of awakening of consciousness.

Several years later, during one of my stays in Bolivia, Raya suggested that on my return to the U.S., I begin a concentrated research project directed at developing some original methods for my societal and cultural peers. This project would begin with one year of concentrated study to target necessary areas of human obstacles, and the following year for the invention of potential methods (tools) for identifying and removing those obstacles. These two years of research would be followed by two years of actual experimentation on both volunteers and myself.

After the first two years, I reviewed my results with Raya. It was clear that the nature of people of affluent western culture had peculiarities not previously prevalent. Their general upbringing and accessibility to multiple forms of *relief,* created, among other things, unique negative emotion patterns, with subtleties never before observed. Although efforts focusing on different aspects of negative emotions had long been a part of work on consciousness, it was clearly necessary to develop some new method that took into consideration the pace and style of western life.

I also discovered that the nature of the pace at which Americans live, as well as their expectation of immediate results, created unique obstacles that required both a revolutionary perspective, as well as new tools for observation and alteration. Similarly, I discovered other areas where what had previously been effective would have to be modified, because the human machine, although basically the same as before, was operating with some very different *fuel.* We both agreed that the results were promising.

I then proceeded into the experimental period. For this endeavor, I enlisted friends and newly-made acquaintances, only a few of whom knew they were involved in deliberate and organized experimentation. During this time, I also began concentrated experiments in group dynamics, including studying what could be achieved by people living and/or working together. Through these early experiments, it became obvious that a certain phenomenon that I called *compartmentalization* was going to take special attention. This I deduced through observation of participants in the experiments who could not easily "escape" from each other, because they lived together, and those who could, because they lived elsewhere. The result of this two-year period was an accumulation of numerous possible unique and original methods and points of view, some of which needed further experimentation and development.

I sought council on how to proceed from Raya, who was then spending some months in Afghanistan at Shahr-e Monjan. I was instructed to spend an extended period of time, one hundred days, in seclusion in the Dasht-e Kavir desert of central Iran, where arrangements would be made for my retreat – after which I should proceed on to Afghanistan where we would meet.

On my eventual arrival at Shahr-e Monjan in Afghanistan, I presented the results of my entire four years of theoretical and practical research to Raya, who participated in this exposition along with five other elder teachers then residing there. The week-long gathering involved my conveying the details and the essence of voluminous notes I had taken. Much translation was needed and animated discussions often lasted late into the night. The conference concluded with a decision that I should initiate formal teaching in America – a decision that Raya informed me of during our return trip to Peru on my route back to the U.S.

This formal teaching, Raya conveyed, should involve application of my past research, in addition to the eventual transmission of the ancient meditation. Raya gave simple instructions of how to go about this task. *Put some posters up with a big picture of your face, and some words under it, and see who shows up.*

In addition, I was admonished not to present myself as more than a step ahead of my students, not to separate or insulate my shortcomings from my students, and to practice, along with them, whatever methods I taught. Raya's final instruction was for me to limit my efforts to people who wanted to change – not that they would necessarily possess the strength to change – but that they should have the wish.

What proceeded was six years of group work on the west coast of the U.S. It was in those years that I developed a telephone relationship with Kurt Gödel, a mathematician and logician, who had worked closely with Albert Einstein at Princeton. He encouraged me to explore the connection between theoretical mathematics and obstacles to human consciousness. With a recommendation from him, I briefly taught a course in Gödel's Incompleteness Theorem at the University of Oregon, focusing more on the incompleteness than the theorem. Using advanced math students as willing participants, we investigated philosophical and spiritual questions, using mathematical uncertainties. It was a fascinating exploration for me.

It was Gödel's opinion, and became mine as well, that solutions to problems, mathematical and otherwise, could best be found by combining as many non-related languages as possible in exploratory formulae. He encouraged my efforts with friendliness and praise, and I genuinely appreciated his brief friendship.

During this period, which coincided with a time of increased interest in alternatives to mechanical life, several hundred people were introduced to these newly developed tools and ideas, and approximately one hundred officially pursued the methods – each according to his or her capacity.

On a trip to Peru toward the end of these six years, Raya asked me to put aside my teaching for a time, in order to check out a phenomenon that was occurring in the U.S. This would require a period of a year or two, in which I would join a particular large and well-organized spiritual group as a member, and try to immerse myself in the experience of their movement.

The facts were the following: A fellow student from Raya's youth, Hans Ji Maharaj – one of those who participated with him in the meditation group taught by Sawan Singh, had died some years earlier, and passed on his teaching authority to his son Prem Pal Singh Rawat, who at that time was seven years old. Prem Pal, now sixteen years old, and becoming known as Guru Maharaj Ji, had in recent years come to England, and even more recently to the U.S., and was, through intermediaries, instructing thousands, with minimal preparation, into the same meditation that was historically presented under very strict circumstances.

Raya asked that I present myself as a seeker along with the other multitudes and, without revealing the nature of my assignment, try to discover, through participation, not deliberation, what was going on. What proceeded was a period of almost two years in which I, following the instructions of Raya, played the part of a "devotee" of Guru Maharaj Ji. Years later, Maharaj Ji altered his program significantly, by requiring a far more extended time of preparation to a much smaller number of aspirants, as well as personally involving himself in the actual instructive process of passing on the meditation.

After this adventure, and following a short hiatus, I re-established my group work in another location. The tools and points of view I presented to those gathered there, new and old, were the refinements of my original research and my six years of work, in addition to the invaluable insights I had gained in my most recent venture with Guru Maharaj Ji.

In the mid-1980s a situation developed in Afghanistan that brought the world of Shahr-e Monjan and my students closer together. Because of the prolonged Afghani war with the Soviet Union, some of the settlements in the remote parts of the country were finding it harder and harder to sustain themselves. Since Shahr-e Monjan was located between Kabul and the Pakistani border – an area of considerable Mujahadeen (rebel) activity, it was often bombed, and the fields that were used for grazing were repeatedly burned. After much postponement, the elders of the school finally decided that it was time to go.

The complex project of coordinating the smuggling out of a number of Afghan refugees, including several of the elders, and settling them in a place that was acceptable, both to the new host country, and the refugees themselves, was undertaken by a multinational group. We sought help from friends of Shahr-e Monjan around the world, and my students and I assisted, not only in raising necessary funds, but also in the actual operation of exiting Afghanistan and relocation. The refugees eventually re-established an abbreviated community in the mountains of South Island, New Zealand, where those few still live today. Their previous mode of functioning has been altered considerably, and they no longer function as a school that accepts students.

Raya the Weaver

In the following year, the school on Lake Titicaca in Peru was also to undergo a drastic upheaval. It had been Raya's opinion for some time, that the focus of work on consciousness should be gravitating toward the United States, and for him to maintain a school in a remote area of Peru would no longer be productive. My attempts to convince Raya to emigrate to the U.S. were not successful, and he, now close to ninety years old, decided to take his last climb in the Andes Mountains that he loved.

Only a few students were left on Lake Titicaca at that time, and it was for them to find for themselves the next step in their personal work on consciousness. Thus, two major centers of learning, one of which had endured for hundreds of years, no longer exist in the places they had previously been. The center of this tradition of experimentation is now to be found in the U.S.

I have just now reread the 82,000 preceding words, and believe that I may have actually planted a fruit tree.

Justin

Epilogue

From time to time everyone needs a reminder of what's really important to them. Sitting in an empty house of worship, taking an ambling walk alone in the woods, lying on your back and looking up at the stars on a warm night, all help a person to return to their center. Of course that return is temporary, and only being filled up from within will truly bring peace.

Until that state of being is within your reach, here are some reminding factors that I have found to be consistent. They are in the form of sayings, books, movies, and songs. Though they may not be what is popularly considered inspirational, they can take you somewhere deep and rich, if you are prepared to look beneath the surface of things – where all real wealth resides. Finding the ones that work for you can be an exhilarating adventure, so bon voyage.

Movies

1) 2001: A Space Odyssey
2) Bronco Billy
3) Contact
4) Joe Versus the Volcano
5) Local Hero
6) The Milagro Beanfield War
7) Powwow Highway
8) The Magus
9) School of Rock
10) Seven Faces of Dr. Lao
11) The Valley (Obscured by Clouds)
12) They Might Be Giants

Books

1) A Story Like the Wind, Laurens van der Post
2) Be Here Now, Ram Dass
3) Childhood's End, Arthur C. Clarke
4) Demian, Hermann Hesse
5) Dreams, Olive Shriner
6) In Search of the Miraculous, P. D. Ouspensky
7) In Watermelon Sugar, Richard Brautigan
8) Journey to the East, Hermann Hesse
9) Lost Horizon, James Hilton
10) Mount Analogue, René Daumal
11) Tales of Power, Carlos Castaneda
12) The Chronicles of Narnia, C. S. Lewis
13) The Last Unicorn, Peter S. Beagle

Songs

1) Sisters of Mercy, L. Cohen
2) Bird on the Wire, L. Cohen
3) Famous Blue Raincoat, Sincerely, L. Cohen
4) Visions of Johanna, Bob Dylan
5) It's Alright Ma, Bob Dylan
6) It's All Over Now Baby Blue, Bob Dylan
7) American Tune, Paul Simon
8) Life Uncommon, Jewel
9) Wot's…Uh the Deal, Pink Floyd
10) Helpless, Neil Young
11) Something Fine, Jackson Browne
12) Angel, Sarah McLachlan
13) Attics of My Life, Grateful Dead
14) Surdas the Gardener, Field & McDonald

The three J. Jaye Gold quotes on the back cover were chosen from many others by the editorial staff at Peradam Press.

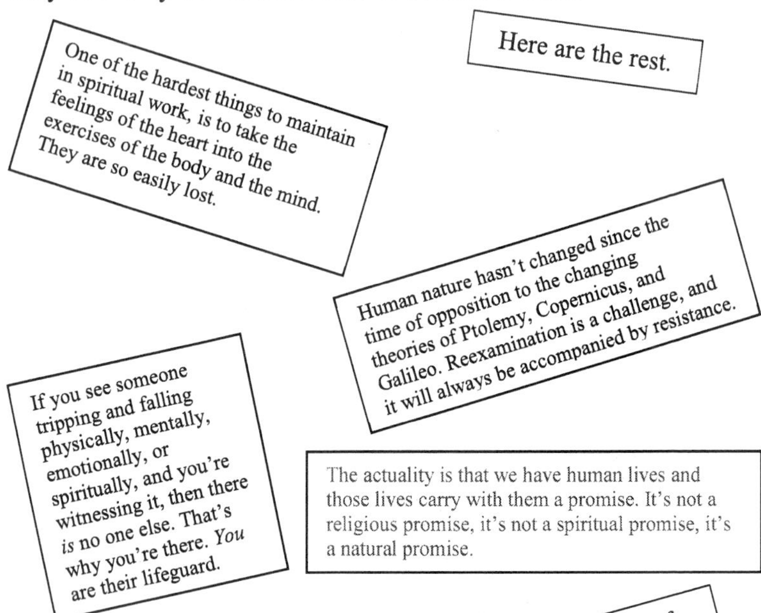

Here are the rest.

One of the hardest things to maintain in spiritual work, is to take the feelings of the heart into the exercises of the body and the mind. They are so easily lost.

Human nature hasn't changed since the time of opposition to the changing theories of Ptolemy, Copernicus, and Galileo. Reexamination is a challenge, and it will always be accompanied by resistance.

If you see someone tripping and falling physically, mentally, emotionally, or spiritually, and you're witnessing it, then there *is* no one else. That's why you're there. *You* are their lifeguard.

The actuality is that we have human lives and those lives carry with them a promise. It's not a religious promise, it's not a spiritual promise, it's a natural promise.

As a servant is filled, only a small bit of what is collected can be kept, And a hero, even less. But to this law there is one exception. If you open up your heart to the universe of love, it will fill you up completely.

You can deceive yourself into feeling the illusion of strength if you surround yourself with people who have not climbed as far as you. You are in good shape compared to them, but you are not in good shape compared to everyone. *It's a long way to the top if you wanna rock and roll.*

Everything we do appears so mundane to us that it's impossible for us to see how focusing on the ordinary could possibly yield an extraordinary experience. Unfortunately, we expect that only extraordinary circumstances will yield an extraordinary experience.

The more intricate the ritual, the more perfection in its performance, the less understanding there is for the original reason for the practice that existed before it became a ritual. The process of the ritual becomes the reality, and the reason that one is doing it, and where it all comes from, disappears.

One of the discoveries from my research, has been that we need not lose the innocence, the inner connection, or the hope with which we began this life. And one of the keys to regaining that purity of heart, is to recognize that it got lost in increments.

We were placed on Earth for some purpose other than to accumulate more. Once we have accomplished the basics, the ones that not all, but many of us already have, then another possibility becomes available.

Our cells look pretty darn spiffy, but they are cells nonetheless. Our lives are extremely limited, although when we compare ourselves to other prisoners, we feel very fortunate. But we are only comparing ourselves to other prisoners – not to free people.

We are terrified of becoming part of the herd because we'll lose something. What we don't understand, is what we fear has already happened. We have relinquished our individuality.

I looked back and saw the fire truck immersed in flames and the red rotating emergency beacon on top was melting. I shouted, "Claude, the truck!" He heard me, turned around, and called back ,"No problem, I've got it under control." Seeing things as they actually are is not so easy.

We have a built-in natural pride that is not exclusive like other prides, because *I am that* and *you are not that*. It is the pride of being a human being. Where does one ever hear that sentiment? It is the only pride that creates no separation between us.

I have proceeded with the premise that, though it is too painful for us to even acknowledge the existence of these diseases of personality in their full-blown form, much less assault them, perhaps their micro-particles are vulnerable to penetration, or at least to scrutiny.

The first requirement, and by far the most important, for anyone who is going to be able to help you spiritually, is that person has to be able to do two things – mail a letter for you, and pass the salt to you. That rules out anyone who is no longer alive – all of them.

The circumstances needed to expand our consciousness are ones that we've already been given. Any attempt to create an artificial world in which to learn is a misdirection. No one could possibly create a world where learning can happen better than the one already created. *Our* job is to not avoid what is in front of us.

45824552R00187

Made in the USA
Middletown, DE
15 July 2017